Intro

Let me start by saying that this is not just a diet. As you probably already know, diets fail. Even if you do lose weight with a diet, you'll gain it back... and lose your sanity in the process.

I see it all the time. I've counseled hundreds of people in the heart of New York City, the melting pot of America. Regardless of age, gender, income, or sanity, everyone has the same problems losing weight because **diets have major pitfalls and blind spots. They don't account for inevitable barriers that stand in the way of their success, every time.**

First of all, **diets don't address your cravings.** If anything they create cravings, and most people have no idea how to handle them. I had one patient admit that she can only stop herself from eating junk food by throwing it in the garbage, then drowning it in bleach and soap. She didn't trust herself not to eat it out of the garbage can. True story.

Another big problem is that people don't stick to their diets when they're stressed. I see it all the time. I have patients who eat because their relationships are failing. Patients who are too exhausted from work to even think about sticking to their diet.

Even if stress doesn't kill your motivation to lose weight, or make you want to eat everything you see, it'll still keep you from losing weight. **Stress hormones make you store fat and prevent your body from letting it go.** Either way, stress is a diet killer.

Another big issue is that **most diets don't account for your body's instinct to *regain* the weight.** Trying to lose 50 pounds in one shot and restricting as many calories as possible might work temporarily, but it'll destroy your metabolism. That's why you always gain the weight back.

Aside from those major barriers, diets don't account for minor details that can either make or break your success. Details that you wouldn't find in research, but that come to the surface when you're counseling people day in and day out.

I have an hour with each patient every week to find out that they're eating too fast, they can't get enough sleep or drink enough water. That their scale isn't positioned correctly, so their weights are inaccurate and making them feel discouraged. Or that they hate how they feel when they weigh themselves, so they avoid it altogether. **A diet won't hold your hand through your weight loss journey and give you solutions to all of those small but significant issues.**

On top of all of that, **everyone's trying to stick to impossible diets.** They're listening to their coworkers who tell them to completely eliminate carbs or their personal trainers who tell them to follow unsustainable meal plans consisting of hard-boiled eggs with steamed chicken and broccoli every day.

I know a guy who tried to lose weight by only eating chicken cutlets that he incinerated in the oven. He did it for months with the idea that it would make him hate eating. But he gained back every pound because it didn't make him hate eating; it just made him hate burned chicken.

I have news for you. **If your diet isn't realistic for you, then it'll fail every time.** You're living in a world full of temptation. It's next to impossible that you'll happily cut out all your favorite foods for the rest of your life, or restrict yourself to 800 calories every day. As soon as you inevitably start eating normally again, you'll gain back every ounce, and then some.

HOW TO LOSE WEIGHT WITHOUT LOSING YOUR MIND

The New Method for Permanent Weight Loss, Mood Control, & Cravings

CASEY KERBS, RDN, CDN

Lucky for you, I have the solutions to all these problems, and they're simpler than you might think.

In this book you'll find:

- **Easy physical and psychological tricks to manage and prevent cravings and overeating.** That way, you can enjoy delicious food (while you lose weight) without being addicted to it.

- **Lessons and tools from experts on how to reduce stress, depression, anxiety, and anger** so that you can feel more carefree and focused.

- **Science-based rules of thumb** regarding what, when, and how to eat to lose weight.

- Tips and guidance on **strength training and cardio exercise**, if you decide to add them into your weight loss plan.

- Scientific strategies to **ensure that the weight you lose stays off for good.**

- Ways to **maintain and restore the health of your gut** because an unhealthy gut will keep you from losing weight.

- A choice between **six different weight loss plans**, so you can pick the one that best fits into your lifestyle.

- **Free downloadable meal plans** with tasty and extremely easy to follow recipes for every stage in your weight loss.

So let's get started. I'm tired of watching you all suffer.

Disclaimer

This book is for just about anyone who's having trouble losing weight. But you should always consult your doctor before making changes, if you have any medical conditions like heart disease, kidney disease, diabetes, or cancer. As a registered and certified nutritionist, I work with all types of medical conditions. But the advice in this book isn't tailored to them. Weight loss generally improves overall health, but there are specific dietary recommendations for specific conditions that aren't covered here. This also isn't for those of you who are pregnant or breastfeeding. Or anyone under 18 years of age. You could still benefit from some of the advice here. But you don't want to lose weight dramatically as you grow. And the caloric recommendations aren't tailored to children, adolescents, and pregnant or breastfeeding mothers.

Part One

Motivation

"You'd think lazy people like me would've been weeded out by natural selection"

-Jim Gaffigan

Before we get into the details of weight loss, I want to make sure you have a realistic goal and that you're motivated enough to get there.

Give Yourself A Break

Some people could care less that they've gained weight, so this doesn't apply to everyone. But, if you're beating yourself up for it, then you need to stop. **We live in a world where nothing is easier than gaining weight. And we have all the wrong ideas about how to lose it.**

You're not the one to blame. You either didn't know how to lose weight, or you didn't care enough to do it. I'm not saying you have to love being overweight. But beating yourself up will just make you unhappy. Which especially doesn't help if you use food as a crutch.

You might think that being hard on yourself is motivating you to make changes. But you'll only make changes that are too extreme, and not sustainable. Then you'll beat yourself up again for not sticking to them. So, try to relax, and give yourself a break.

Figure Out Why You Want to Lose Weight

In the past your attempts to lose weight have obviously failed. Otherwise you wouldn't be reading this. **You might think that it was because you were too weak or too lazy. But it could've been that you actually didn't care enough when it mattered the most.**
It's easy to feel bad about yourself and decide to lose weight when you're trying on tight jeans. But that's not when you need motivation. You need it when you're deciding what to eat for lunch, or whether or not you'll eat the leftover cookies in the break room. At that point it's easy to convince yourself that your weight is fine. **Your desire to eat something that tastes good can easily outweigh**

your desire to lose weight if you don't have a solid reason for putting in the effort.

You'll need to think seriously about how losing weight will impact your life in a way that you actually care about. Something you can remind yourself of when you have a choice between something that'll help you lose weight or something that'll make you gain.

That reason should feel like a desire, not an obligation. Otherwise it'll never outweigh the desire to eat whatever you want. Trying to lose weight "because the doctor said you should" is not a desire. And losing weight because you feel fat might be depressing. Below are some examples of positive motivations for losing weight. **Figure out what feels the most inspiring to you.** Think of what's going on in your mind when you find yourself wanting to lose weight and remind yourself of that when you're lacking motivation.

Positive Motivations to Lose Weight
- To stay healthy and active as you get older
- To get off of medication
- To get rid of joint pain
- To have a healthy future pregnancy
- To get in control of your cravings
- To feel good without using food as a crutch
- To feel attractive and comfortable in your body

Focus on Fat Loss

I always have patients who pick a number out of thin air and decide that they *must* be at that weight. The problem is that they aren't taking body composition into account. Meaning, how much weight loss is coming from muscle and how much is coming from fat. You want the weight that you lose to be coming from fat, and *not* muscle.

That's because muscle cells burn a lot of calories, even when you're sitting around, doing nothing.

The more muscle you have, the more calories you burn throughout the day. Not only that, extra body fat isn't healthy. Fat cells send out inflammation into your body that causes damage and leads to diseases like cancer, diabetes, heart disease, and Alzheimer's.

So, you're best bet is to make your weight goal based on fat loss. Which could make your weight goal much less extreme, because fat is very light compared to muscle.

If you ever look at a picture of ten pounds of fat, you might be surprised at how much that actually is. Losing only ten pounds of fat makes a big difference in your health and how you look.

For example, I used to obsess about being 110 pounds. I'd restrict way too much and end up looking like a skeleton. By that point, I had no muscle left. And I was desperate for whatever food I was restricting. Every time I lost that much weight; I'd almost immediately gain it back. I just blamed it on a lack of willpower, like we all do. But I eventually realized that getting down to that weight was pointless. All I did was lose muscles and willpower. Now I'm 120 pounds, less fat, more muscle, and I eat more now than I ever did.

If you focus on fat loss, then you might be relieved to see that you don't have to lose as much weight as you originally thought. And by preserving your muscle, your body will burn more calories. In other words, you can eat more without gaining weight. We'll talk more much more about preventing muscle loss and how to measure your body fat in Part Seven. For now, if you want, you can use the reference below to help you figure out your body fat percent goal.

RANGES OF BODY FAT PERCENTAGE

	MEN	WOMEN
Unhealthy	Less than 10-12%	Less than 2-4%
Athletic	14-12%	6-13%
Fit	21-24%	14-17%
Healthy	25-31%	18-25%
Obese	More than 32%	More than 26%

Break Down Your Goals

If your weight goal is too overwhelming, then break it into smaller parts. Your ultimate goal could be getting down to 150 pounds and 25% body fat without feeling like you would kill for a slice of pizza. But that starts with smaller goals like losing a pound a week and getting more sleep. **You don't have to think of everything all at once.** It's like climbing a staircase; you need to take one step at a time. Just one pound a week turns into 50 pounds in a year.

Be Patient

Losing weight takes patience and persistence, not extreme effort. If you restrict what you eat and exercise *a lot*, then you'll lose weight fast. But it won't last for long. You'll end up losing motivation, gaining it back, or plateauing at that weight for weeks.

Some people are impatient, which is understandable. They'd rather lose seven pounds a week than one or two. They don't listen to my advice, and they try to lose weight fast. They eat less and exercise more than I tell them to. And they're very pleased in that first week, when they've dropped five pounds. But after a week or so they gain it back and have to admit that I was right. So, do yourself a favor and be patient.

A Little Effort Goes A Long Way

Some people are the opposite of the impatient go-getters. Their weight stays exactly the same because they don't want to make any changes. No matter how small those changes are. I remind them that they won't be putting in effort for the rest of their lives. You can lose five to 16 pounds in just a couple of months. By that time, the changes you made will be a habit. And once you reach a weight that you're happy with, you can eat *more* than when you were losing weight.

Think of How Good You'll Feel

There'll be times when you need some extra motivation to keep you from eating midnight snacks or to get yourself off the couch and head to the gym. **When you're feeling lazy, it's easy to forget why you wanted to lose weight in the first place. When that happens, it helps to think about the outcome of your effort. Instead of the effort itself.**

Try to picture yourself at your goal weight and comfortable in your body. Or how you'll feel when you see your weight drop the next morning. That feeling can inspire you to work towards it.

Have Some Faith

If I have a new patient that can't get motivated, I'll ask them if they actually believe that they can lose the weight. Surprisingly, a lot of them say no. **Some people are so used to struggling with their**

weight, that being thin turns into an unattainable desire. Rather than an actual goal.

It makes sense, though. If you've never hit your goal weight, then you might not actually believe you can. You might not be able to picture it happening. If you don't believe you can lose the weight, then you'll get easily discouraged by little slip ups. You'll chalk it up to the fact that you just can't do it.

If you actually believe you'll lose the weight, you won't take those slip ups so seriously. You're much more likely to realize that it's just part of the process. And that you'll do better next time. So have some faith. Especially because you're doing things differently this time.

Don't Wait for The Perfect Time

I can't tell you how many excuses I hear every day. Of course, I'm sympathetic, but it's almost as if people are just looking for an excuse to indulge. Recently a patient told me that she was so frustrated about missing her hair appointment that she needed to get a milkshake. As if this was an unavoidable sidetrack.

Your weight loss plan won't be hard. But it'll take consistent motivation to reach your goal. If your motivation disappears every time there's a bump in the road, then you'll never get there. **Don't keep waiting for the perfect time to stay on track, because it'll never happen. Stressful situations will recur like clockwork, and they'll knock you off track every time if you let them.** You can't keep using them as an excuse to lose motivation.

There's a time and a place to enjoy all the foods you like, but your plan won't work if you need to use food as an emotional crutch. **In the next section we'll work on ways to manage mood and anxiety so that you don't need to use food to feel good.**

Part Two

Cravings, Emotional Eating, And Overeating

"Food is like drugs. Except you can't just stop eating cold turkey, because cold turkey is delicious."

-Comedian at the Comedy Cellar, NYC

You're Not Weak, You're Human

Almost every new patient that comes to my office complains about their lack of willpower like it's a character flaw. They expect to be able to constantly deprive themselves for the rest of their lives, which will never happen. What they don't understand is that their brains are hardwired to crave, and it has almost nothing to do with who they are. **In order to feel like you're in control, you need to learn how to work around your natural instincts to indulge.**

You can enjoy good food while you lose weight, but there are some limits. And no matter how motivated you are, there will still be times when it's hard to stop yourself from overindulging. Especially when you're at a restaurant, and one part of your brain is telling you to eat every piece of bread in the basket. Even though another part of your brain is telling you not to. The part of your brain that's urging you to eat the bread is called the "reward center." It can easily overpower the other part of your brain that's trying to keep you on track.

The reward center is strong, because it's built for survival. It's designed to give you pleasure for doing things that keep you alive. Like eating.

In the past, eating bread triggered your reward center to release dopamine, which made you feel good. And the reward center remembers that. **When you see the bread basket, the reward center lights up and triggers dopamine in anticipation of the bread.** *Then*, **it releases stress hormones to make you feel bad. You feel like the dopamine you'll get from eating bread is the only way to feel better. This is why it's so hard to resist food when it's right in front of you.**

The reward center makes you crave food, even if you aren't hungry. It urges you to keep eating, even if you're full. And it builds up a tolerance to the dopamine it gets from food. Which makes you want to keep eating more and more, until you feel the same "high" that you got the first time. But you'll never really feel satisfied. It usually takes willpower or a stomachache to make you stop.

The reward center isn't going anywhere. But it helps to understand that it's the cause of all your cravings and overeating. It'll help you realize that you aren't weak, you're just human. The next time you have a craving, take note of how you feel. **It isn't just the taste that you crave. It's the survival part of your brain, tricking you with stress hormones and dopamine.**

Brain Hacks and Habits to Prevent Cravings and Overeating

Of course, you'll want to indulge sometimes, and you don't have to feel bad about that. Later on, we'll cover "cheat days" and indulgent foods that fit into your meal plan. But **you don't want to be in a position where you feel powerless against your cravings or your desire to overeat.** In this section, we'll work on removing a lot of the factors that lead to cravings and overeating. Like stress, dehydration, and lack of sleep. Plus, ways to deal with cravings once they come up.

Stay Hydrated

Feeling thirsty is actually a late sign that you're dehydrated. **At first, dehydration can come out as a craving for food.** Make sure you're drinking enough water to prevent those cravings. And before you decide to indulge, drink some water first and see if your craving gets weaker.

Aside from regulating your appetite, you need to drink enough water to digest your food and for almost every other function in your body. If you're not drinking water because you don't like the taste, then remember that it's life sustaining water. It doesn't have to taste like a milkshake. But if you really can't stand it then **try flavored seltzer or adding lemon, lime or other fruit. Or get flavored herbal cold brew tea bags to add to your water.**

If you're used to drinking juice and soda, water's going to seem boring. It'll take some getting used to but cutting out flavored drinks can save you a few hundred calories a day and a pound of fat a week.

If you don't like cold water then try naturally caffeine-free tea like rooibos, chamomile, peppermint, or flavored herbal teas. If you don't drink enough fluids because it's inconvenient for you to use the restroom then try to hydrate when it's convenient, like first thing in the morning.

How Much to Drink

If you're drinking enough fluids, your urine should be clear at least once a day. You'll feel clearer headed, energized, and have less cravings. Keep track of your water intake a few times to see if you're drinking enough. To figure out how much you need you can follow these general guidelines or calculate it on your own with the steps below.

GENERAL HYDRATION NEEDS

	MEN	WOMEN
CUPS	12 Cups	9 Cups
OUNCES	96 Ouces	72 Ouces
LITERS	3 Liters	3 Liters

Hydration Equation

Step 1

Divide your bodyweight in half for how many ounces of fluid you need in a day.
Example: 150 pounds divided by 2 = 75 fluid ounces a day

Step 2

About 20% of your fluid comes from the food you eat, leaving the other 80% of your needs from fluids. So you can then calculate 80% of your total fluid needs.
Example: 75 fluid ounces x .80 = 60 fluid ounces from fluids a day

Step 3

Divide that number of ounces by the size container you usually drink from.
Example: 60 fluid ounces divided by 16.9 fluid ounce water bottle = 3.5 bottles a day.

Eat Enough

How many times have you tried to lose weight by restricting yourself as much as possible, just to gain it all back? It's the most common and damaging weight loss mistake. The problem is that your body is designed to survive a lack of food by holding onto your fat stores for dear life. It doesn't know the difference between a diet and a famine.

When you restrict too much, your body won't readily give up your life sustaining fat stores. It'll actually do the opposite. Your body adapts to less food by slowing down your metabolism. It starts using less food for energy and storing more of it as fat for later. On top of that it'll increase your appetite so that you overindulge whenever more food becomes available again. And the problem with a diet is that you aren't actually starving, so there's almost always plenty of food available.

Luckily there's a way to lose weight without triggering those fat-saving and craving-inducing survival instincts. **Later, you'll learn how much you should be eating and other ways to prevent cravings and a slow down in your metabolism.** You'll probably be surprised to see how much you can eat, while still losing weight.

Don't Get Too Hungry

You might be proud of yourself for being able to ignore your hunger, or suppress it all day with caffeine, gum and water. But that's not helping you lose weight. I'll explain this in more detail later. For now, just know that **during your eating window you shouldn't wait until you're very hungry before you eat something. Instead, you should always eat whenever you *start* to feel hungry.** We'll discuss eating windows in the next section.

If you haven't already noticed, it's impossible to eat an appropriate portion size or make a healthy choice when you're starving. I know that some of you don't eat lunch until you're about to pass out, so that you have less time at work after your break. If you're one of those people, then you should at least **keep a snack at your desk like a piece of fruit to have when you start to feel hungry. Or carry them with you when you're out of the house so there's no excuse to let yourself get too hungry.**

Get To Know Your Early Hunger Signals

If you're used to ignoring your hunger signals, then you might not know what they feel like. Early hunger signals aren't the same for everyone. It can start by feeling like your stomach is empty. And it can be very subtle and sometimes only last for a minute or two. If that's the case, then it's easy to ignore. Especially when you're busy. But pay close attention to that feeling, because that's when you should start to eat. Otherwise you'll end up feeling like you're starving out of nowhere.

If You're Always Hungry

The first hunger signals of the day will start about 12 hours after dinner the night before. Then, three to five hours after each meal throughout the day, and one to two hours after a small snack. If you feel like you're hungry more often, then it could be from a lack of sleep, medication, stress, not eating enough, or eating processed carbs or inflammatory foods. We'll cover what to eat, how much to eat and sleep later on, which will help regulate your hunger.

If You're Never Hungry

Having no hunger signals is not a good thing. It makes it hard to know when you should start eating, and when you should stop. If you never feel hungry then it could be from ignoring those signals. If you ignore hunger signals for long enough, then your body won't keep bothering you with them. You can even lose your hunger signals from having extra body fat, because fat cells send out a hormone that suppresses your appetite. It could also be that you're suppressing your hunger with things like caffeine, nicotine, gum, or medications.

If you're not doing anything to suppress your appetite but you *still* never feel hungry, then start by making a routine eating pattern. Losing weight and having some regularity will start to trigger your hunger signals.

Wait Until You're Hungry

If you started eating out of boredom or because of a craving, then there's no clear reason to stop eating. But **if you start to eat when you're hungry, then you're more likely to stop eating when you feel full or satisfied.** If you do have a craving, then at least try to wait until you start to feel hungry before you eat.

Eat Slowly

It takes a while for your brain to get the signal from your stomach that it's full. That's why if you eat too fast, then you can put away a lot of food before you even start to feel full.

If you eat slowly, your brain has time to get the signal that your stomach is filling up. You'll feel full with much less food.

If you're used to eating fast, then use the guidance below to help you slow down. It's not easy at first, but it'll become a habit after a while. I've seen plenty of fast-eaters turn into the slow-eaters. And they're appalled to realize how fast they used to eat, and how much they could eat in one sitting.

How to Slow Down

1. Don't wait until you're starving to eat. Eat when you just start to feel hungry.
2. Take a few deep breaths before you eat and when you notice that you're starting to eat fast again.
3. If you notice you're chewing fast and lost in your thoughts, then refocus on breathing, chewing, and tasting your food.
4. Make sure you chew each bite *thoroughly*. Remember that you can't properly digest food that hasn't been thoroughly broken down.

5. Take small bites so that it's easier to chew the whole mouthful before you get tired of the taste.
6. Put your food or utensil down between bites.
7. Focus on the food in your mouth, not the food on your plate.
8. A lot of times fast eating is because of stress. The next section will help to improve your mood and alleviate stress which will naturally slow down your eating rate.

Stop Eating When You're Comfortably Full

When you finish eating, you should feel comfortably full. **If you don't feel full at all, then you'll end up craving something else. But if you feel stuffed, then you most likely ate too much.** And stretching out your stomach actually triggers hormones that *increase* your appetite.

If you tend to overeat, then follow the guidance below. Once you start to eat smaller portions, your stomach won't shrink but it'll actually get less stretchy. You'll have a hard time eating big portions again, and you'll always feel satisfied with less food.

How to Prevent Overeating

1. Pre portion your food. As a survival instinct, your brain will urge you to eat everything in sight.
2. If you're at a restaurant, throw your napkin on your plate to cover your food when you feel satisfied, or ask for a to-go box with your meal and take whatever's left over.
3. Stand up and walk away from the food or put it away when you feel satisfied. If you keep looking at the food, you'll want to keep eating it.
4. Have a meal ender like a cup of tea, a hard candy, or a chocolate covered mint. Or brush your teeth, chew gum, or use mouthwash to cleanse your pallet.

Set Aside Time to Eat

Set aside around 15 to 20 minutes to eat each meal. Once you do this, you might be surprised to see that you've actually been inhaling your food in less than five minutes. If you're eating your food this quickly, then you'll never feel full.

You should set aside time to eat, even if you're a slow eater. **If you take too long to eat, then you'll never feel full because the food is emptying out of your stomach at the same slow rate that it's going in.** The same thing happens if you're just taking a few bites here and there while you're doing other things. I'm not saying that you can't eat while you watch TV. But if you do, then take your time to chew your food thoroughly and don't take long breaks between each bite.

Pay Attention to What You're Eating

If you're distracted when you're eating, then you can easily eat an entire bag of chips without even enjoying it. You might not even realize what you were doing until there are no chips left. At that point you won't feel satisfied with the snack, even if you're full. Because **mental satisfaction from eating is even more important than how full you are.**

Once again, I won't say that you can't eat while you do anything else. You can still pay attention to what's in your mouth while you sit in front of the TV or computer. When you eat, chew thoroughly, and pay attention to tasting and breathing. You'll probably have to keep reminding yourself at first, but it'll become a habit.

Imagine Being Satisfied

Sometimes you might be lost in the pleasure of eating and be surprised and disappointed when there's no more food left. Then you'll look for something else to eat, even if you're full.

While you eat, imagine feeling satisfied when you finish. And *expect* **to feel satisfied.** It'll help you prevent that abrupt end of pleasure when you finish. If you know that you always want a little something after your meals, then you can factor that into your meal plan. Or use a low-calorie meal ender like tea, a hard candy, or chocolate covered mint.

Trick Yourself with Seconds

If you're the type of person that doesn't feel satisfied with one serving, then break your meals up into two portions. Have ¾ of your meal at first, and then serve yourself the rest as a second portion. **It'll make you feel like you're eating more, even if it's the same amount of food.**

Don't Eat Boring Food

If your food is bland then you'll end up hating your diet. **There's plenty of room for flavor in your weight loss plan**. If you do your own cooking, then you can use the recipes from the free meal plans on my website (crkwellness.com) or from other sources. If you always order take out or if you usually go to restaurants, it's not like your only option is boiled chicken and vegetables. You can get something indulgent that fits into your calorie range. Just include some vegetables, even if you're getting them as a side.

Fit in A Treat

You don't have to feel guilty if you're not ready to give up daily junk food. There's always a way to fit something into your plan.

Knowing that there's a treat scheduled into your day will help you avoid each temptation that comes along.

Distract Yourself

Your brain's reward center can be triggered whenever you see, smell, or think about something pleasurable. You know when someone gives you a treat or there're snacks in the break room? You weren't craving anything before, but now you feel deprived if you don't have it.

If you want to avoid indulging or overeating, then your best bet is to distract yourself and get it out of sight. If you're still craving it, then *don't* talk to yourself about it. Even if it's to tell yourself *not* to eat it.

If you're thinking about it, you'll keep wanting it. Because your reward center is still being triggered by the thought of the food.

As soon as the craving comes up, focus your attention on something else until it goes away. Distract yourself with anything, like watching something funny, talking to someone, listening to music, taking a walk, drinking tea, or even meditating, which we'll cover later in this section. The craving won't last forever.

Don't Say "I Can't"

If you tell yourself you *can't* have something, it'll make you want it even more. And the truth is, you *can* have indulgent food and still lose weight. Just not all the time. So be very careful with your thoughts. If you want a double cheeseburger, don't tell yourself you *can't* have it. Change the thought to something like:

"I could have that now if I want. But I'd rather eat something healthier. I can have a treat later if I want, but it's not worth it right now."

Don't Say "I Have To"

Don't tell yourself that you *have* to eat healthy. If you *have* to do something, it implies that you don't *want* to. And, it's not true. You might have to go to work, so you don't get fired. But there's no immediate consequence from eating a cheeseburger instead of a salad.

Change the thought to something like:

"I'd rather have a salad so I can get some nutrients and feel full without going over on calories".

Once you finish eating and you feel full, the desire will be gone or at least not as strong.

Stop Feeling Guilty

You won't be perfect all the time, and you don't have to be. Sometimes you might overeat, or get off track for a few days, which is normal. **Feeling guilty and beating yourself up is just a way of telling yourself that you're not in control.** But that's not the case. You're just in the process of making new habits.

Instead of beating yourself up, take note of how you feel. Overeating doesn't feel good. Neither does getting off track and gaining a few pounds. If you remember how that feels, you'll be much less likely to do it again in the future.

Don't Romanticize Unhealthy Food

Be more realistic with how you think about foods like cookies and pizza. Whatever your "weaknesses" are. Notice how they actually taste, and how you feel while you're eating them. **It's not the taste of the food that's creating the feeling. The reward center of your brain is tricking you with dopamine, making you feel happy.**

It'll make you think about the food like you're actually in love with it. You'll be associating those foods with the taste, the reward it gives your brain, *and* love. So, resisting them is even harder. Yes, the food tastes good, but tone it down a notch.

Understand How Food Affects Your Health and Mood

You might see cake and doughnuts as "unhealthy food". But in reality, it should barely be considered food at all. Your body doesn't know what to do with it. Food is what comes out of the ground, perfectly designed to fuel your body. It has the nutrients that your body *needs* every day. Your body uses those nutrients as tools and building blocks to make feel-good hormones like serotonin and dopamine. Along with every other chemical that allows your body to function.

Meanwhile, junk food is lacking those nutrients. And it triggers inflammation, which causes a lot of problems in your body. Inflammation affects the part of your brain that's responsible for motivation and anxiety. And it even reduces dopamine and serotonin. So, **unhealthy foods will make you anxious, lazy, and unhappy in the long run.** Inflammation also disrupts the hormones that suppress your appetite. Eating inflammatory junk food ends up making you hungrier. And chronic inflammation is the underlying cause of diseases like cancer, heart disease, diabetes, and Alzheimer's.

Don't think of healthy food as a way to deprive yourself of a good time. And don't think that eating vegetables once a week is enough to reverse the damage you've done for the last two decades. The nutrients in natural foods are what your body needs to function *every day* to keep you from being fat, sick, lazy, and anxious. Not to say you have to be perfect all the time. Full disclosure, I wrote this section while I was eating leftover pizza and Cookie Crisps. But whatever, it's a cheat day (we'll go into more on that later). Just try to eat *mostly* natural foods.

Make New Associations

Whether or not you realize it, you've made associations with different foods throughout your life. Those associations affect your choices. **If you have a hard time choosing something healthy then it's probably because you think of it as a form of self-discipline.** If you always think of healthy food that way, you'll never enjoy it. If you don't enjoy it, you won't choose it.

But you're forming new associations with healthy food, now that you understand the positive impact it has on your mood, health, and waistline. It's not like you're going to feel the same way about a salad as you would a bowl of pasta. But you'll appreciate it much more than you used to.

At the same time, your association with junk food is changing. Before, you probably thought of it as the "forbidden fruit", which makes it even more desirable. But now you understand that nothing is off limits. There's always a time and a place to indulge. And when you have a craving, you realize that you don't just want it for the taste. The craving is from the reward center of your brain, tricking you with dopamine and stress hormones. This new association with cravings and junk food will make them easier to resist.

Set Up Healthy Triggers

Throughout the day, you'll come across plenty of triggers for junk food. Like vending machines and advertisements. They trigger your reward center to remember the dopamine it gets from it. Luckily, they won't be as powerful, now that you associate them more with addiction, disappointment, and deteriorating health and mood.

Now that you have some positive associations with healthy behaviors, you can start to trigger them in the same way. Your brain will remember the reward it gets from seeing things like your weight drop on the scale and the endorphins you get from exercise. So, **keep things like your scale, healthy snacks, water, or gym clothes in sight.**

Try Going Cold Turkey

Cutting out junk food altogether works for some people, but not everyone. It's worth a try if you feel like you're ready to do that. **Foods like sugar, pasta, bread, and dairy are addictive to your reward center. If you eat them once, you'll want another fix.** Not having them for a few days can reduce your cravings, once they're out of your system. In the meantime, you can use some of the alternatives in the next section or try to swap out processed sugar for natural sweeteners like honey, agave, or maple syrup.

Try Healthy Alternatives

You can try healthier alternatives to foods like chips, cookies, cake, ice cream, muffins, pasta, and candy for the times that you have a craving but don't want to go overboard. Most of the alternatives aren't packed with artificial flavors or sugar so they're less damaging to your health and less likely to trigger cravings. Below are some alternative products, and you can visit my website (crkwellness.com) or other sources for healthy alternative recipes.

HEALTHY ALTERNATIVE PRODUCTS

SALTY	SWEET
Tolerant Red Lentil, Green Lentil, or Black Bean Pasta Bada Bean Bada Boom Snacks Rhythm Beet Chips Rhythm Kale Chips Pop Chips Skinny Pop Veggie Straws Pop Corners Hippeas Chickpea Puffs	Laughing Giraffe Organics Snakaroons Emmy's Organics Coconut Cookies Soozy's Muffins Barnana Organic Chewy Bites Nothin But! Cookies Yasso Frozen Greek Yogurt Bars *Halo Top Ice Cream *Enlightened Ice Cream *Dreyer's Whole Fruit Bars

NO CALORIE

Republic Of Tea Caramel Vanilla, Caramel Apple, Strawberry Chocolate
Celestial Cinnamon Apple Spice, Black Cherry Berry, Honey Vanilla
Tazo Dessert Delights Tea
Flavored Seltzer
Shirataki Noodles

*contains artificial sweeteners

Get Enough Sleep

If you don't sleep enough, you'll feel hungrier than usual the next day because of your body putting out the hunger hormone ghrelin. You'll end up feeling the need to eat more than what's usually satisfying to you.

Studies also consistently show that getting less than seven hours of sleep a night causes weight gain and poor health. Unfortunately, not everyone has time for that. And some of you will say that you can get five hours of sleep without feeling tired. But that's probably with the help of caffeine. Some studies show that there's a small percentage of people that don't need as much as eight hours of sleep. But it's not common.

You should get somewhere between seven to nine hours of sleep each night. Especially if you're having trouble with cravings or if your weight loss is at a plateau.

Tips for Better Sleep

If you have trouble falling asleep or staying asleep, then try the tips below. But remember to be patient. Worrying about the fact that you can't fall asleep will only make it harder.

#1 Relax

- Practice meditation throughout the day and especially before bed. See the section on meditation for more guidance.
- Use lavender oil in a diffuser or spray it on your pillow.
- Buy a weighted blanket to sleep with.
- Give yourself a massage or acupressure described below.
    - With your fingertips, apply pressure between your eyebrows, right above the nose, the depression between your first and second toes, or on top of the foot, for a few minutes until you feel a dull ache.
    - Just inside your ear, press down. Don't go inside the ear and puncture your eardrum.
    - Massage both of your ears for a minute.

#2 Make Yourself Tired

- Try to force yourself to stay awake or keep your eyes open for as long as you can.
- Do something or think about something boring. Try doing simple math problems in your head.
- If you're lying in bed for more than 30 minutes and you're still not tired, get out of bed and do something boring, like a puzzle or a coloring book.

#3 Make Your Room Dark, Cold, And Quiet

- Use earplugs or listen to relaxing music with headphones.

- Use an eye mask or keep your room as dark as possible. The dark cues your brain to produce melatonin which helps you sleep. Any light can interfere with this and keep you awake.
- Keep your room cool. Low body temperature is important for sleep. You can take a warm shower before bed and the cool air will reduce your body temperature when you get out.
- Splash your face with cold water for 30 seconds.
- Take a break from artificial light close to bedtime. Use candlelight or low light and avoid the light from your phone or other devices for at least an hour before bed. You can also put a night timer on your phone that dims the light at whatever time you choose.

#4 Avoid Alcohol, Caffeine, And Water Before Bed

- Drink most of your fluids earlier in the day to avoid waking up during the night to use the bathroom.
- Avoid alcohol as much as possible, as it can lead to insomnia. Check out Allen Carr's book *Quit Alcohol Without Willpower* for more help on this.
- Limit caffeine throughout the day. That includes coffee, supplements, energy drinks, and caffeinated tea. Some people are very sensitive to caffeine. If you're having trouble sleeping and have tried everything else, avoid caffeine altogether. If you need a natural energy boost, make sure you're fully hydrated and try the energizing breathing exercise below.

Energizing Breathing Exercise

1. Inhale to the count of two
2. Exhale to the count of two
3. Inhale to the count of two
4. Exhale to the count of three
5. Inhale to the count of two
6. Exhale to the count of four

7. Inhale to the count of two
8. Exhale to the count of five
9. Repeat a few times, then return to your normal breathing.

#5 Make A Routine

- Set a bedtime for yourself based on when you need to wake up for the next day.
- Use a sleep tracker like Fitbit, ora, or Apple watch.

Check with Your Doctor

If you have trouble sleeping, wake up feeling unrested, or tend to snore then check with your doctor to find out if you have sleep apnea. It's a condition that causes interrupted breathing while you sleep. Sleep apnea is a catch-22 because it's caused by being overweight, and it makes it harder for you to lose weight. It's dangerous because it increases your chances of having a stroke or a heart attack. But it's treatable and reversible. There are devices you can wear while you sleep to help you breathe, until you lose enough weight to reverse it.

Lift Your Mood and Alleviate Anxiety

You'll have a hard time losing weight if you need to use food as an emotional crutch. That can be as innocent as snacking on nuts at your desk to get you through the rest of the day. But it can get a lot worse than that. I've had plenty of patients admit to popping Oreos like Xanax or eating an entire box of doughnuts when they're depressed.

Anxiety or a bad mood will always affect the way you eat. It'll make you binge, crave, or even lose your appetite so that you don't eat enough. And it's happening to just about everyone. Before

I see a patient, I ask them to rate their level of depression and anxiety on a scale from one to ten. And I rarely get back ratings that are below a four in either category. I've actually only had one patient out of hundreds that told me he's honestly happy. It was so shocking to hear that I found myself wondering if something was wrong with him.

There are more than three million cases of anxiety diagnosed every year, starting at age six. And three million cases of depression diagnosed every year, starting at age three. That means you're as likely to have a mood disorder as you are to catch a cold.

Regardless of their prevalence, most of us have never learned how to deal with mood disorders. School doesn't teach stress management and neither do most of our parents. It's up to you to learn new ways to manage stress, without food.

I've been through this myself. Fortunately, I learned how to get rid of anxiety and panic attacks that left me too scared to leave the house, and depressive episodes that kept me in bed for days at a time. I learned it all after I realized that binge eating, antidepressants, and anti-anxiety medications are not the solution.

I'm not a psychologist but I get my advice from experts. It's helped a lot of friends and patients become happier and more relaxed, get rid of anxiety, panic attacks, bad moods, and disordered eating.

The following is just an overview of concepts that'll help you get on a better path. They're the topics that come up most often, but there's much more to learn about. At the end of the section are other resources and books I recommend if you're looking for more guidance.

The Influence You Have Over Your Mood

Emotions are caused by chemicals in your body called hormones and neurotransmitters. Some make you feel good, and some make you feel bad. There are different factors that can affect these chemicals, like diet, exercise, puberty, menopause, genetics, gut health, and environment. But **one of the biggest influences on these chemicals are your thoughts.**

Negative thoughts trigger hormones like cortisol that make you upset, anxious, unhappy and uncomfortable. Positive thoughts *reduce* those stress hormones, and instead they trigger hormones like serotonin that make you feel good. You can even do an experiment to see how that works. Repeat something negative to yourself and see how it makes you feel. Then do the same thing with something positive.

It's important to understand that your *thoughts* trigger these chemicals, so that you can start taking control over them. **A lot of people ignore the control they have over their mood, or they're unaware that they have control.** It seems like circumstances or people are the cause of stress. But they aren't. Your *thoughts* about the person or the situation is causing the emotional reaction.

Of course, you could say that if it wasn't for that person or that situation, you wouldn't be thinking something negative. And depending on the situation, it might feel impossible to avoid feeling or thinking negatively. But you do have a choice in the matter. You don't *have* to continue thinking negatively. The only person it's hurting is yourself.

The Damage of Negativity

Negative thoughts don't just make you feel bad. They trigger stress hormones that:

- Slow down your brain coordination.
- Reduce your ability to process information and solve problems.
- Disrupt the regions of your brain that are responsible for mood, memory, and impulse control.

Therefore, negativity makes you stupid, unhappy and impulsive.

And worst of all, **negative thoughts *rewire your brain* in a way that makes you more prone to being negative**. Because your brain creates new connections in your brain like neurons and synapses to support whatever you focus on.

The Benefits of Positivity

Unlike negativity, positive thinking affects your brain in a good way. **It triggers chemicals like dopamine and serotonin that improves your ability to think, learn, solve problems, and pay attention.**

In the same way that negative thoughts rewire your brain to think negatively, **positive thoughts rewire your brain to think optimistical**ly.

It's not realistic to say that you should never have a negative thought. But understand how destructive, addictive, and pointless negative thoughts are. They'll make you feel bad, eat more, and prevent you from focusing and solving problems. Once you understand that, you can decide to adjust your thoughts, to adjust your mood.

I get how it sounds. It's like having someone telling you to just cheer up. It's the last thing you want to hear. But it's in your best interest to do so.

Say you have an issue with your partner. Or you have a million projects due at work. Continuously stressing about it will solve nothing. It'll just make it impossible for you to think clearly, focus, and come up with a solution. **Finding a way to relax will trigger chemicals that get your brain working at full capacity.**

Adjust and Refocus Your Thoughts

There are two ways to get rid of negative thoughts. You can either change your perspective or take your focus away from them altogether.

Changing your perspective and adjusting negative thoughts can feel like brainwashing yourself. It doesn't seem natural when you first try to replace negative thoughts with something positive. At first you might need to **steer them in a more neutral direction**.

If you're telling yourself that your life is a mess, then it'll be hard to convince yourself that everything is perfectly fine instead. It'll feel like too much of a stretch. But you might be able to tell yourself that things are okay, they could be worse, and that they'll get better. Changing your thoughts from negative to neutral will start to lift your mood. Once you've gotten used to that, it'll be easier to replace neutral thoughts with ones that are actually positive.

If you're having trouble coming up with something positive, then **remind yourself of what you're grateful for**. It's physically impossible to feel unhappy while you're feeling grateful.

If work is stressing you out, then remind yourself that you're grateful to have a job. If there's traffic on your commute home, then be grateful to have a place to come home to.

It also helps to have some **go-to phrases or mantras**. That way you can nip the negative thought in the bud, before it spirals you into a bad mood.

If you're running late or your plans were ruined, it's easy to get frustrated. Instead of gritting your teeth every time, you can use the mantra **"Everything happens for a reason."** Because really, you don't know what could've happened if things *did* go as planned. You might've been at the wrong place at the wrong time and got hit by a bus!

Other times, you might try the mantras
- All is well
- Being happy is my first priority
- This negative thought is not important, and not worth it

If it's too hard to adjust, then refocus.

When you feel stress building up, you can decide that it's not worth holding onto the negative thought. Then refocus your attention.

It's okay to let yourself get out of your head by doing something productive, watching TV or standup comedy, doing something creative, going outside and getting into nature, giving yourself a massage, listening to music, reading, exercising, or socializing.

But for some people, all the distractions in the world are not enough to refocus your thoughts and get out of your head.

If you've never exercised your brain's ability to focus, then it won't be easy to do so on command. **In order to strengthen your ability to focus, you should learn to practice meditation, which we'll cover in the next section.**

Meditation is learning to guide your attention to a focal point like your breath, every time a thought enters your mind. Doing this on a regular basis will make it easy for you to refocus your attention away from negative thoughts. It'll help you get more present to the moment in whatever situation you're in.

The more focus you have on the moment, the less focus you have on negative thoughts.

But even if you do meditate, it's still easy to get lost in thought throughout the day. When you notice that you're unfocused, anxious, and stuck in your head, then snap yourself out of it by getting yourself into the moment. You can do that by **focusing your attention on your breath, and on anything that you can see, hear, touch or smell.**

Stop Reaching for Happiness

The idea that you shouldn't search for happiness is not widely accepted by people in the modern world, but I'll try to explain it anyway.

Constantly reaching for things to make you happy will *prevent* you from being happy. Searching for something is not relaxing, and happiness is only possible when you're relaxed.

People are always searching for things like relationships, money, and power, to feel happy. And it doesn't work. How many people in the world are hopelessly miserable regardless of their wealth or relationships?

Your ability to be happy depends on your ability to feel relaxed and present in the moment. If you can't do that, then you'll never be able to enjoy any of the things that you're searching for. Being with your ideal partner, living in a beautiful home and traveling to your dream location won't make you happy if you can't get out of your head.

That's not to say that you shouldn't have goals and desires. It just means that you should learn to be present so that you can enjoy all the things that you've worked for.

Prioritize

It's easy to lose sight of what's really important in your life when you have rent due, your behind on all your projects at work, and your family is driving you up a wall. Instead of prioritizing your mood and giving yourself time to relax or appreciating what you have, you spend your time stressing over every flaw in your life and everything you need to accomplish.

But what would be important to you if you found out you'd die tomorrow? Not the argument you had with your spouse or how much money you have. You'd wish you hadn't wasted so much time being unhappy about things that are ultimately insignificant. You would wish that you'd have appreciated everyone and everything in your life instead of taking it for granted.

At least once a day, remind yourself of what's really important. Prioritize feeling happy and relaxed so that you don't waste all your time and energy stressing over things that don't really matter.

Let Yourself Feel Better

If you're having a hard time using this advice, then make sure you actually want to. **A lot of times people stay unhappy because they aren't letting themselves feel better.**

It could be that you're getting sympathy when you complain, you see yourself as someone who's always stressed, you feel like you can't be happy until you accomplish something. It could be that you feel guilty or not worthy of being happy, or maybe you're so used to thinking about something that it's hard to stop.

It could take some time to let go of negative thoughts. But you have to decide what's more important. Holding onto the negative thoughts that are harmful to your mood and your brain function or letting them go so you can think clearly and be happy.

Don't Be So Hard on Yourself

I'm in a position where I see how people really treat themselves. They beat themselves up over little things and tell me how fat and lazy they are. How disappointed they are in themselves for getting to this point.

They treat themselves like garbage. They don't see how talking down to themselves is like spending all their time with someone who wants them to be unhappy. It's like being stuck in a toxic relationship.

Start to pay attention to how you talk to yourself. You might notice that you're talking to yourself in a way that you would never tolerate from anyone else. In a way that you wouldn't talk to a friend or someone that you care about.

If you notice that you're being hard on yourself, then work on being nicer. It might feel uncomfortable at first, but it'll become second nature once you get used to it.

Quit Raging

If you're mad at someone or something, then your best revenge is not to be angry. Anger triggers those same stress hormones that shut down brain function and make you feel bad. That doesn't mean you should never get angry. But it does give you a reason not to *stay* angry.

Especially because you'll probably need to confront someone or solve a problem. **With all those anger induced stress hormones, you'll be in no position to solve problems or communicate.**

If you're angry with someone then calm down before you talk. Swallow your pride and use all the empathy you can manage to see where the other person is coming from. Recognize that no one is perfect. You're much more likely to get your point across if you're calm and thinking clearly.

In other situations, you might not have the opportunity or authority to communicate. In that case it's not worth holding onto the anger. The only person it's hurting is yourself.

If you're angry with a situation and there's something you can do to change it, then it's in your best interest to calm down so that you can find the best solution.

Slow Down

Rushing around is an easy way to trigger stress hormones. You might have a limited amount of time to get things done, but **there's no point in running around like a chicken with its head cut off, if it's going to make you anxious, forgetful and unfocused.**

Try to avoid situations that cause you to rush. Give yourself a few extra minutes whenever possible. But be aware of your thoughts and mood if you're short on time. **It's possible to move quickly without being frantic, if you:**

- Don't agonize about the consequences of being late, if there's nothing you can do about it.
- Let yourself be a few minutes late, if there are no major consequences.

- Find useful ways to spend the time that you're sitting in traffic or waiting for the bus or train, like listening to music, audiobooks, reading, meditating, or just relaxing.
- Take a minute to calm down when you start to feel rushed and unfocused.

There are inevitably going to be times that you're running around. But make sure you don't keep that same frantic energy going for the rest of the day. When everything's settled, set aside time to reset with a quick meditation or a few deep breaths.

Believe That You Can Change

Having anxiety or depression is not a life sentence, and it doesn't always require medical intervention. I've seen a lot of people become a whole new person, just by changing the way they think and deal with stress.

Sometimes the biggest and most difficult step towards being happy is to decide that you don't want to be unhappy anymore. To make that possible, understand that you have the power and the tools to be happier if you decide to make that change.

Accept the Highs and Lows

Even after you make these changes, there will still be times that are harder than others. Some days or some weeks that you feel less happy than you were before. If you notice that happening, then don't worry about it. Stressing about being stressed will only make things worse. Just know that as long as you keep applying these techniques, things will start to get better again.

The Impact of Gut Health and Diet on Your Mood

Although thoughts have a large impact on your mood, it's not the *only* determining factor. The food you eat and the health of your digestive system plays a large role in how you feel.

You might eat junk food to feel better but it's doing you more harm than good. Processed, high carb, high sugar, and high fat foods increase inflammation in your body. Inflammation reduces the availability of feel good hormones like serotonin and dopamine, making you feel worse in the long run.

The food you eat also impacts the level of inflammation and the type of bacteria living in your gut. Which is incredibly impactful on your mood. The digestive system is not just a place to absorb food. It's actually seen as the largest endocrine organ in the body. **With the help of the right bacteria, your gut produces much of the hormones in your body. Including the feel-good hormone serotonin.**

An unhealthy gut with the wrong bacteria will prevent your body from producing the hormones that are essential to your mental and physical health. In the next section we'll cover ways to improve your gut health.

Get Some Help

If you need more help, **consider cognitive behavioral therapy**, which helps you unlearn patterns of thinking and behaviors that cause anxiety, depression and addiction.

Other Books That Can Help

If you don't want therapy but you still need more help, then try reading some of these books. You can pick ones that are specific to your biggest source of stress, or about happiness in general. For your convenience, you can find them all for purchase on Amazon.com through my website (crkwellness.com).

Relationships and Confidence

Loving What Is, by Byron Katie
The Honeymoon Effect, by Bruce H. Lipton
Why Men Don't Listen And Women Can't Read Maps, by Allan and Barbara Pease
Art Of Seduction, by Robert Greene
The Way Of The Superior Man, by David Deida

Career

Think And Grow Rich, by Napoleon Hill
The War Of Art, by Steven Pressfield
Mastery, by Robert Greene
How To Win Friends And Influence People, by Dale Carnegie
4 Hour Work Week, by Timothy Ferriss
Pitch Anything, by Oren Klaff
Flip The Script, by Oren Klaff
Crucial Conversations, by Patterson, Grenny, McMillan, and Switzler

Happiness

Joy: The Happiness That Comes From Within, by Osho
Power Of Now, by Eckhart Tolle
Radical Honesty, by Brad Blanton
The Four Agreements, by Don Miguel Ruiz
Be Happy, by Robert Holden

Practice Meditation

The general idea of meditation is that you're setting aside a few minutes every day to quiet your mind and to let go of everything.

In the beginning, it'll take a lot of practice to let go of the constant chatter but it's the best thing you can do for yourself. To lose weight, be happy, more relaxed, and more productive. It might make you feel like you're thinking clearly for the first time in your life.

Unfortunately, there are a lot of misconceptions about meditation. After months of resistance, I had a patient admit to me that she hadn't tried it yet because she heard it would open her mind up to evil spirits. I spent the rest of the session convincing her that she won't get possessed.

I have other patients who've never tried it because they thought they'd have to sit Indian style on the floor and chant mantras. But that's definitely not the only way.

There are a lot of different ways to meditate, and you don't have to be a hippie to do it. In fact, **almost all of the 200 industry leaders interviewed in Tim Ferriss' book *Tools of the Titans* meditate every morning.**

On a personal note, I'll admit that meditation has single handedly transformed my life. Long gone are the days of procrastinating, losing focus, feeling anxious, or looking to food for comfort. It's given me so much more control over my thoughts and emotions.

I know how essential it is to being happy and sticking to a weight loss plan so I urge everyone I know to make it a habit. Even though a lot of people are skeptical.

I have a high-strung patient, who could never get her cravings in check. Stress would always get in her way, just like everyone else. She told me that I sounded crazy for suggesting meditation. But after a year of convincing, she finally tried it. And now it's her lifeline. She shuts the door to her office every day to meditate and won't look up from her desk until she's finished. Since she's made it a habit, she dropped right down to her goal weight and hasn't needed any help to stay there. Hopefully, you take my advice sooner than she did.

How Meditation Helps with Cravings, Overeating, And Emotional Eating

Increased Dopamine

When you have a craving, it's because your reward center is looking for pleasure in the form of dopamine. But it doesn't necessarily need chips or cookies. Meditation triggers the release of dopamine in the same way as food, drugs, or shopping. But it's not fattening or expensive.

Improved Focus

Sometimes when you have a craving, you need to focus on something else until it passes. Otherwise, you won't be able to stop thinking about the food until you eat it. Meditation helps by strengthening the neural pathways that are responsible for focus. Which makes it much easier to steer your mind away from the craving or the negative thoughts that are causing it.

Improved Mood and Relationships

Meditation has been shown to alleviate depression and anxiety by increasing dopamine and shrinking the part of the brain that's responsible for negative and wandering thoughts. It also improves your ability to communicate and makes you more empathetic, which naturally improves your relationship with friends, family, partners, and coworkers. Tension in any of those relationships is a common source of stress. With an improved mood and improved relationships, you're much less likely to use food as a crutch.

Improved Awareness, Memory, and Cognition

Meditation changes the structure of your brain in a way that improves awareness, memory and cognition. Which helps in a lot of ways. Having more awareness will keep you from ignoring your hunger signals. Which usually leads you to be starving by lunch time and making bad decisions. Improved awareness can prevent you from snacking mindlessly, eating too quickly, and ignoring the fact that you're already full.

An improved memory will prevent you from doing things like forgetting to bring your lunch or afternoon snacks to work. Which is an unexpectedly common barrier to weight loss. Improved cognition and memory will also make you more efficient at work, which will inevitably reduce stress.

Prevent Eating Out of Boredom

One of the most common barriers to weight loss is wanting to eat when you're bored. Usually we try to fill in down time with TV, eating, drinking, or scrolling through our phones. Anything to keep us from being bored, thinking about our to-do lists, or letting our minds conjure up any negative thoughts it can find.

Sometimes even those distractions aren't strong enough if you're too stuck in your head. After you've been meditating for some time, your mind will be quieter, and it'll be easier to focus and enjoy those activities.

Practicing meditation will also give you something productive and enjoyable to do with your down time.

Improved Sleep

Not getting enough sleep will make you more hungry than usual. And it's common to use food for energy when you're feeling tired. Meditating before bed, or on a consistent basis, will help you fall asleep and stay asleep throughout the night.

Tips for Meditation

The Basics

When you meditate, you're setting aside time to let everything go. In the beginning that won't be easy. You'll need to repeatedly guide your focus towards something like your breath or a sound, and away from your thoughts. The goal is for it to feel good, reduce stress, and improve your focus and clarity. Everyone goes about it in a different way. Some people listen to guided meditations on the train or in their office. Others lie in bed or sit on the couch with a candle lit. However and wherever you choose to meditate doesn't matter. It's all based on your preference. The guidance below will help you figure out what works best for you.

What to Expect

During each meditation, you might only feel that your mind was clear for a few seconds. Especially in the beginning. But even that's enough to start feeling the effects. Meditation will make you feel happier, calmer, and more focused. If you keep it up, you'll notice that it gets a lot easier to focus away from your thoughts, which'll make you feel even better. By the end of each session you might feel a kind of high which is the dopamine that's triggered by meditation.

Refocus Without Judgement

When you start to meditate, you'll notice that your thoughts are emerging and wandering without control. Every thought you have is causing an emotional reaction and preventing you from being relaxed and present to the moment. So, you'll use a focal point like your breath to focus away from them. Whenever you start to notice that you're lost in thought, gently steer your attention back to your focal point.

This might be hard at first, but don't get frustrated. Getting frustrated or putting yourself down will defeat the purpose of the meditation. It's only difficult to focus because the region of your brain that's responsible for wandering thoughts is overdeveloped from years of using it. And your ability to focus is underdeveloped from a lack of practice. The more you practice meditation, the easier it'll be to steer your focus.

Don't Obsess About an Empty Mind

It's hard to feel good if your thoughts are all over the place. But your mind doesn't have to be completely empty for you to benefit from meditation. What's more important is that it makes you feel good. Even if that means that you're just focusing on positive thoughts or visualizations. So, don't be discouraged or distracted if you don't have an empty mind.

Find What Feels Good

Granted, there'll be times that you can't be as comfortable as you'd like. Sometimes you'll only have a chance to meditate on the train or in your office. But you'll want it to be as enjoyable as you can make it. You can use scents from candles, essential oils or incense, wear comfortable clothes, lay down with a blanket over you, shut off the lights, or play relaxing music. Some people find it more enjoyable to sit up straight or meditate while they walk, stretch, or give themselves a massage. Whatever works for you. Don't be afraid to experiment until you find what feels good, and switch things up if you're getting bored.

How to Breathe

How you choose to breathe depends on how stressed you are when you start. If you're stressed or very anxious when you begin, then a controlled breathing technique can help you relax. It'll trigger your body to switch from your "fight or flight" nervous system to your "rest and digest" nervous system. Once you feel relaxed, the meditation will be more enjoyable. There are a number of breathing techniques to use. Two of the most effective are described below. You can start with them, and then continue the meditation while you breathe naturally.

4-7-8 Breathing Method

1. Place the tip of your tongue against the ridge of tissue behind your upper front teeth and keep it there through the exercise.
2. Exhale completely through your mouth, making a whoosh sound.
3. Close your mouth and inhale quietly through your nose to a mental count of four.
4. Hold your breath for a count of seven.
5. Exhale completely through your mouth, making a whoosh sound to a count of eight.
6. Repeat the cycle three more times for a total of four breaths.

2-4 Breathing Method

1. Inhale through your nose for a count of two.
2. Hold the breath for a count of one.
3. Exhale for a count of four.
4. Hold the breath for a count of one.
5. Repeat until you feel more relaxed.

What to Do If Your Heart Is Racing or Skipping A Beat

Stressful or exciting thoughts can make your heartbeat quickly, which can be scary and make it hard to relax. Getting nervous or frustrated about your heart rate will only make it beat even faster.

I've had patients go through this, and I've been through it myself, so I know how to help. At one point when I didn't think I was even under much stress, I developed what the doctor called a mitral valve prolapse which is very common. It makes you feel like your heart is missing a beat and then trying to catch up by beating fast. It made me scared to meditate because I wanted constant distraction from that feeling. But going so long without meditation only made it worse. The doctor wanted me to get all kinds of tests done and wear a heart monitor. But I read that it could be caused by stress, so I decided to try and fix it before I spent hours getting tests done. And it actually worked. In one shot I got it to disappear completely, and it never came back.

First of all, you have to recognize that your heart is racing and acting strange because of your thoughts. You have to realize that you have complete control over the movements in your body. Prove this to yourself by breathing very purposefully. Try opening and closing your hands while recognizing that it's your brain that's controlling these movements. It might sound a little crazy, but it works.

Your heart rate will slow down when you stop worrying about it and focus on something positive and relaxing. You can slow your heart rate down even further with the breathing exercise below. If you keep having this problem, then consider reducing or avoiding alcohol or caffeine and other stimulants in your diet. You should still consult with your doctor if you're noticing any abnormalities in your heart.

As a side note, magnesium supplementation has been used to treat mitral valve prolapse. You can fix it without any supplements but if that doesn't work for you then you could ask your doctor about magnesium.

Breathing Exercise to Slow Down Heart Rate

1. Take a breath in.
2. Hold it for a few seconds.
3. Breath out through your mouth as slowly as possible.

Eyes Open Vs Eyes Closed

Keeping your eyes open or closed depends on how you're meditating. If you're doing it while you walk, then I would suggest you keep your eyes open. But for the most part, you can open and close them as you please. Sometimes closing your eyes will help you relax, but other times it can make it harder to get out of your head. Do whatever feels natural and comfortable for you.

Pick A Focal Point

Whenever you start to notice that you're lost in thought, gently steer your attention back to your focal point. Experiment with the focal points below until you find something that works for you, and switch things up if you're getting bored with your routine. Keep in mind that you can use more than one at a time. For example, you can use a breathing exercise while you listen to music.

Guided

Guided meditations make it easier for some people to get out of their head. Sometimes, the person's voice can be annoying, or you might find it too dramatic, or distracting. Take some time to find ones that you like. I would recommend you use Insight Timer because it's free and has a lot of options.

Apps
1. Insight Timer
2. Headspace
3. Breathe
4. Oak
5. Binaural Dream
6. H*nest Meditation

Sound

Music, natural sounds, and binaural beats can be used to trigger relaxation or positive emotions. But it can also be distracting. You might find that you prefer silence or whatever noises you can hear from outside your window. The following apps have many different sounds to choose from.

Apps
1. Breathe
2. Insight Timer
3. Binaural Dream

Visualization or Open Eye Focal Point

You can visualize an object, shape, or relaxing environment to steer your mind away from any distracting thoughts. You can even keep your eyes open and focus your attention on an object. Then close your eyes and try to visualize the object in your mind.

Breath

Breath is the most common focal point to use. You can use it at the same time as mantra, body scan, sound, active, visualization, and guided focal points. As mentioned before, controlled breathing techniques can be used to trigger relaxation if you're not already relaxed. Once you feel relaxed, you can focus your attention on the feeling of your breath. There are different ways to do this. Like focusing on the feeling of your breath as it moves through your nose or mouth, and how your stomach moves up and down as you breathe. Or you can think of how you're inhaling oxygen and exhaling carbon dioxide. Only do this if you find that it works for you, as it can be distracting for some people, causing them to breathe unnaturally.

Mantra

There are plenty of mantras to use for meditation. You can come up with your own or find one online. It can be in English or another language. Pick ones that feel positive, without stirring up a lot of thoughts. Mantras can be said out loud or silently repeated in your head. To start, you can try "SO" as you breathe in and "HUM" as you breathe out. Or repeat simple phrases like "All is well", "I feel good", "Be here now", "I am present", "I am grateful", etc.

Active

If you have trouble sitting still then you can do something with your body while you meditate, like walking, stretching, coloring in mandalas, or using meditation balls. Walking on a treadmill works well because you can hold onto the sides, listen to music, and walk carefully with your eyes closed.

Body Scan

Lie down or sit up straight and breathe naturally as you individually relax all the muscles in your body. Start from your feet and work your way up to the top of your head, or the other way around. If you find this difficult to do on your own, then you can search online for guided body scan meditations.

Timing

Experiment with the timing of your meditation. For instance, when you wake up, before you leave for work, on your commute, at lunch, when you get home, or right before bed. You'll probably find that there's a time you prefer. Meditating in the morning will keep you focused and relaxed throughout the day, while meditating before bed is the most helpful for sleep. You can start off with a few minutes at a time and work your way up to 15 minutes. You can try for 30 minutes or even an hour if you'd like. You'll get the most benefit if you meditate on a daily basis for about 10 to 15 minutes. You can spread it out throughout the day. Meditate for a few minutes in the morning, on your way to work, during the day, and before bed, so you can feel the positive effects all day.

End on A High Note

There'll usually be highs and lows throughout the meditation. At one point you might be feeling positive and clear headed. But then you get distracted by a train of thought that leaves you feeling negative. If your timer goes off at that point, then give yourself an extra minute or two to clear your mind again. That way the meditation will leave you feeling good.

Keep It Up

People always tell me that they couldn't meditate because they were too stressed. It's easy to make that excuse for yourself, but it doesn't really make sense. If you made meditation a priority, then you wouldn't be so stressed. And time restraints are no excuse either. You can always find a few minutes in the day to meditate if you try. Even one minute would make a difference.

You might even stop meditating for the opposite reason. Regular meditation will have you feeling better on a daily basis, so you might feel like there's no need to keep doing it. If that's the case then it's fine to fall off for a day or two, but you should get back to it before long. Don't wait until you're completely stressed out before you start again.

You might also be tempted to stop when it seems like it isn't working as well as it used to. That can happen when there's more than usual on your mind. If that's the case, then it might take a little more time or effort to refocus. But it could be that you're just getting bored with your routine. So, don't hesitate to switch things up with different sounds, breathing exercises, activities, scents, or guided meditations.

Part Two Summary

Question Yourself

It's not that you should never indulge. You should enjoy food. But food isn't that enjoyable when you're using it as a vice or turning to it because of an uncontrollable compulsion.

The next time you notice yourself eating fast, craving, or eating too much, ask yourself why. Figuring out the reason will help you decide how to avoid the compulsion.

- If you're stressed, try to meditate. Or do something that'll help you relax.
- If you're bored, then find anything to occupy your time until you feel hungry.
- Drink water to figure out if dehydration is causing the craving.
- If you're tired, then take a break from what you're doing, drink water, lay down if you can, or use one of the energizing breathing techniques from the section on sleep.

- If you're hungry then eat a satisfying and balanced meal.
- If you're just being triggered by the sight of something, then distract yourself until the craving passes.

The New Normal

In the past, you habitually reacted to boredom, stress, fatigue, and dehydration by eating. That conditioned your brain to crave food whenever you felt any of those triggers. So, at first it'll take some effort to stop yourself from automatically reacting, to question the reason for the trigger, and to act in a different way. But once you've done that a few times, it'll break the conditioning, and form new automatic reactions to boredom, stress, fatigue, and dehydration. Then there'll be much less effort involved.

Part Three

How to Lose Weight and Keep It Off

"I don't stop eating when I'm full. The meal is not over when I'm full, the meal is over when I hate myself"

-Louis CK

This section explains the concepts you need to understand about how your body lets go of fat. So that when you choose a weight loss plan in the next section, you'll know what I'm talking about instead of blindly following my advice.

Eat While Your Metabolism Is Running

You've probably heard that you shouldn't eat past a certain time of night. There's some truth to that, but the cut off time has more to do with your body's internal clock than the actual time of day.

Some things in your body happen once every 24 hours, and for a limited amount of time. Like sleep, digestion, and metabolism. Your body isn't designed to sleep all day, and it isn't designed to process food all day. **Your body will only properly digest and metabolize the food you eat for about 12 hours a day.** The clock starts as soon as you ingest anything but water, and it stops about 12 hours later.

If the first thing you eat or drink is at 9:00 am, then you wouldn't want to eat anything after 9:00 pm. Preferably even a couple of hours before that, because you still have to digest after you eat.

If you eat for more than 12 hours a day, then you're more likely to be overweight and develop metabolic disorders. You should try to minimize your eating window to 12 hours a day at most, which is easy to maintain as long as you're getting 7 to 8 hours of sleep. If you're up all night, then you'll end up getting too hungry to stop yourself from eating. We'll cover eating windows in more detail when you choose a weight loss plan.

You Have to Burn Sugar Before You Can Burn Fat

Your body stores the energy that it gets from food as fat and as glycogen. Glycogen is basically stored sugar.

Before your body can start burning fat, it has to use up your glycogen stores. **Your body uses up glycogen stores when you restrict calories and exercise**. We'll cover how much you should be restricting and how to exercise later on. Because you do *not* want to restrict calories as much as possible.

Another way to use up glycogen and start burning fat is to fast for more than 12 hours.

As long as you don't eat or drink anything with calories, then your body will use up your glycogen stores in about 12 hours. After that, it'll start burning fat for as long as you continue fasting.

If you fast for 16 hours a day, then you'll have about four hours a day that your body is burning fat for energy. The first 12 hours of the fast is burning glycogen, and the last four hours are burning fat.

I'll get into the specifics of how to fast later. But you don't have to fast in order to lose weight. Every weight loss plan is different.

Only Suppress Hunger If You're Fasting

A lot of people think they're burning fat when they skip lunch or wait until they finally get home before they eat. They think that being hungry for two hours is helping them lose weight. But it's not.

Again, it takes 12 hours without eating before you actually start to burn fat.

If you eat breakfast at 9:00 am and then wait six hours until 3:00 pm to eat lunch, you're not burning fat. You're just making yourself hungry for no reason. That'll make it impossible to eat slowly and control your cravings.

During your eating window, you should eat whenever you start to feel hungry.

Get to Know Your Early Hunger Signals

If you're used to ignoring your hunger signals, then you might not know what they feel like. They aren't the same for everyone. It can start by feeling like your stomach is empty. It can be easy to ignore and only lasts for a minute or two. But once you start to pay attention and eat at the first sign of hunger, they'll be more noticeable.

If You're Always Hungry

The first hunger signals of the day should start about 12 hours after dinner the night before. Then, three to six hours after each meal, and one to two hours after snacks. If you feel like you're hungry more often, then it could be from lack of sleep, medication, stress, not eating enough, or eating processed carbs or inflammatory foods. Later, we'll go over what to eat and how much to eat, which'll help to regulate your hunger.

If You're Never Hungry

Having no hunger signals is not a good thing. It makes it hard to know when you should start eating, and when you should stop. If you never feel hungry then it could be from ignoring those signals. If you ignore hunger signals for long enough, then your body won't keep bothering you with them. You can even lose your hunger signals from having extra body fat, because fat cells send out a hormone that suppresses your appetite. It could also be that you're suppressing your hunger with things like caffeine, nicotine, gum, or medications.

If you're not doing anything to suppress your appetite but you *still* never feel hungry, then start by making a routine eating pattern. Losing weight and having some regularity will start to trigger your hunger signals.

Don't Eat When You're Not Hungry

If you're not hungry, your cells don't need energy. That means anything you eat at that point will be stored as fat and glycogen that you have to burn off later. Try to wait for your hunger signals to kick in. If you're having a hard time waiting, then refer back to Part Two on cravings.

Hit Your Caloric Sweet Spot

Almost everyone is under the impression that they should eat as little as possible to lose weight. But that doesn't work. If it was humanly possible to maintain that kind of restriction, then everyone would be skinny. But clearly that's not the case.

Restricting as much as possible will make you to lose weight fast for about a week or two. But your body gets used to that very quickly. **Your body will adjust to extreme restriction by slowing down your metabolism, using your muscles for energy, and increasing your appetite.** That's why almost everyone plateaus and gains weight back when they restrict too much.

There's actually a caloric "sweet spot" for weight loss, and it's determined by your resting metabolic rate, or RMR. Your RMR is how many calories you need to survive in a completely rested state. The calories you need to do things like breathe and pump your blood.

You burn a few hundred calories more than your RMR every day just by being awake, walking around, and thinking.

If you consistently eat just enough to support your RMR, then you won't slow down your metabolism, lose muscle, or increase your appetite. But you will lose fat because you're still burning more than you're taking in by moving around throughout the day. You'll burn even more than that if you decide to exercise.

Unfortunately, I have a lot of patients who fight me on this.

They try to restrict as much as possible, because they know they'll lose weight fast if they do. But they ignore the fact that they *always* gain the weight back immediately once their appetite ramps up. Which it always does. And they're only focusing on the number on the scale. Once I show them their body composition, they get to see that the weight was coming from muscle, not just fat.

You might get impatient or overly enthusiastic and want to restrict more. But you're much better off eating the right amount every day, losing one to two pounds a week, feeling satisfied, maintaining your metabolism, and keeping your muscles. Eating less than your caloric sweet spot for even a day or two is enough to slow down your metabolism and interfere with weight loss.

As you lose weight, your RMR will gradually decrease, and you'll adjust your calorie target accordingly. There'll be more on that in Part Five. Not every weight loss plan relies on caloric intake, but it's good for everyone to have an idea of how many calories they need.

Balance Your Meals

Unfortunately, you won't get ideal results from only eating pizza and ice cream every day. It's not that you have to eat perfectly all the time. Because you *could* lose weight regardless of what you eat, as long as you're hitting your calorie target. But eating junk every day will definitely wreak havoc on your health, gut, and mood. **For the most part you should eat nutritious meals that have protein, non-starchy vegetables and slow digesting carbs.** Below are examples and benefits of those food groups, you can get specific recipes and meal plans from my website (crkwellness.com).

Protein

You need protein in your diet to maintain muscle. They're also typically slow to digest, so they'll keep you full. You can get protein from animal sources like **eggs, meat, fish, or poultry**. Or from plant sources like **quinoa, grains, beans, lentils, nuts, or seeds**. You can use soy products, but they're usually processed and genetically modified. Go for **organic tofu, tempeh** or **edamame**. For animal products, it's best to choose organic because they're free from antibiotics, growth hormones and appetite stimulants. For beef and milk, the best quality is from grass fed cows.

Slow Carbs

Yes, you can eat carbs and still lose weight. If you don't eat *enough* carbs, your body will turn the protein you eat into carbohydrates anyway. That means you won't be able to use that protein to maintain your muscle.

The only time you should try to cut out carbs is if you're following a strict ketogenic diet. But I don't recommend it. The idea of the ketogenic diet is that it causes your body to use fat as a sole source of energy. People do lose weight with this diet. But it takes a lot of diligence to strictly remove carbs from everything you eat, which usually isn't sustainable. Completely eliminating foods usually leads to an intense desire for them. That'll cause you to binge on them or at least feel deprived.

That being said, not all carbs have the same effect on your body. **You want most of the carbs you eat to be slow digesting, like quinoa, beans, legumes, teff, bulgur, buckwheat, brown rice, millet, kamut, oats, squash, fruit, or plantains**. **Sweet potato** and **white potato** are fine too, in moderation. Carbs that dissolve slowly will keep you full longer. They'll distribute sugar into your blood more slowly. Meaning your cells have time to use the sugar for energy. As opposed to foods like pasta, bread, white rice, sugar, and soda, which digest quickly and distribute sugar into your blood all at once. Your cells can't use all of that energy at one time, so the excess sugar is stored as fat.

It's not that you can never have pasta or bread again, but it's something to work on limiting.
Look back to the section on *Healthy Alternatives* for products that mimic your favorite carbs without the high sugar load.

If you're a vegetarian you can double up on beans, lentils, and quinoa because they'll count as your carbohydrate *and* protein.

Fat

The fat in your diet should be coming from **lean meat, fish, avocado, and a little bit of extra virgin olive oil**. Other oils are usually processed with chemicals, even if they aren't listed in the ingredients. Keep in mind that **fatty foods like avocado, nuts, seeds, and nut butters are high in calories, without doing much to fill your stomac**h. They're healthy, but if you're a smaller person that doesn't have many calories to work with, then they're not your best option.

Non-Starchy Vegetables

A third to a half of your meal should be non-starchy vegetables. They'll fill you up with almost no calories. And they tend to be anti-inflammatory and packed with antioxidants, so they'll improve your health and mood and regulate your appetite.

Non-starchy vegetables are **green leafy vegetables, asparagus, eggplant, artichokes, beets, brussel sprouts, carrots, celery, cucumber, cabbage, cauliflower, mushrooms, onions, turnips, peppers, radishes, string beans, tomato, and zucchini.**

Starchy vegetables like corn, peas, potatoes, and yams *don't* count towards the vegetable part of your meal. They have a lot more calories and would count as the carb part of your meal.

Keep Your Gut Healthy

Your gut hosts a hundred trillion bacteria and other microscopic bugs. You actually have more microbial DNA than human DNA in your body. Research is showing that there's an important link between the type of microbes in your body, and your likelihood of being overweight. **Hosting and supporting the growth of the wrong bacteria can actually make you gain weight.**

There are a lot of factors that influence the type of bacteria that live in your body.

- Urban areas breed a lot of unhealthy bacteria. Living in the city makes you more likely to have problems with your gut.
- Taking antibiotics kills off healthy bacteria in your body, leaving room for unhealthy bacteria to populate.
- Being born through a c-section means you were never exposed to a lot of the healthy bacteria you needed.

- Eating a diet high in fat and sugar and low in fiber will feed unhealthy bacteria and starve off healthy bacteria.

You're not doomed if you didn't have a natural birth, live in the city, or if you've ever taken antibiotics. The right diet, supplements, activity, and reduced stress levels can impact your gut bacteria in a way that can help you lose weight.

Diet

High fiber foods like fruits, vegetables, beans and legumes feed healthy bacteria, and foods that are high in fat and sugar feed unhealthy bacteria.

The following foods are called prebiotics, are particularly good at supporting healthy bacteria.

- Leeks
- Asparagus
- Chicory
- Artichokes
- Garlic
- Onions
- Wheat
- Bananas
- Oats
- Soybeans

The following foods contain healthy bacteria however, they usually don't contain high enough doses to drastically alter your bacterial profile, so you might want to consider taking probiotic supplements.

- Kefir
- Kimchi
- apple cider vinegar

- Sauerkraut
- Kombucha
- Miso

If you have digestive issues, then those foods and supplements can be bothersome. Especially if you have chronic bloating. You would need to heal your gut before taking probiotics or eating some of those fiber rich foods which we'll cover next.

Supplementation

You don't need to take probiotics to lose weight, but there are a lot of studies that show significant weight reduction from probiotic use. According to Consumer Lab, three strains of bacteria are particularly effective. Bifidobacterium breve, and Lactobacillus gasseri for both men and women. And Lactobacillus rhamnosus for women in particular. Check with your doctor before you start taking any supplements, because they're not regulated by the FDA. But these specific products have been rated and tested by Consumer Lab for purity, contamination, and digestibility.

For your convenience, you can purchase these on Amazon.com through my website (crkwellness.com).

Recommended Probiotics for Men and Women

Hyperbiotics Pro-15
Vegetarian, Non-GMO, Free from Yeast, Lactose, Soy, Iron, Gluten, Wheat, Nuts, Preservatives, Sugar, and Artificial Colors or Flavors. Timed-release.

Ingredients: Proprietary Probiotic Blend [L. plantarum, L. fermentum, L. acidophilus, B. infantis, L. casei, B. longum, L. rhamnosus, B. lactis, L. reuteri, L. salivarius, L. paracasei, L. gasseri, B. bifidum, B. breve, S. thermophilus] 5 Billion CFU, Prebiotic Fructooligosaccharides (FOS) 25 mg. Other Ingredients: Microcrystalline Cellulose, Hydroxypropyl Methylcellulose, Pectin, Stearic Acid, Sodium Carbonate, Guar Gum, Turmeric.

Probiotic for Women

Garden of Life® Dr. Formulated Probiotics Once Daily Women's
Vegetarian, Non-GMO, Free from Gluten, Dairy, and Soy.

Ingredients: Women's Daily Probiotic Blend [[Lactobacillus acidophilus, Lactobacillus plantarum, Lactobacillus casei, Lactobacillus paracasei, Lactobacillus bulgaricus, Lactobacillus brevis, Lactobacillus reuteri, Lactobacillus salivarius, Lactobacillus fermentum, Lactobacillus gasseri, Lactobacillus rhamnosus] Total Lacto Cultures (40 Billion CFU), [Bifidobacterium lactis, Bifidobacterium bifidum, Bifidobacterium breve, Bifidobacterium infantis, Bifidobacterium longum] Total Bifido Cultures (10 Billion CFU)] 248 mg] Total Probiotic Cultures 50 Billion CFU, Organic Prebiotic Fiber Blend [Organic Potato [Resistant Starch] (tuber), Organic Acacia Fiber (A. senegal)] 377 mg.

Exercise

Even low intensity exercise changes the shape of the gut and blood flow to the gut in a healthy way. It also supports the growth of healthy bacteria. Even if it's just low intensity. A lack of exercise will do the opposite, having an unhealthy impact on your digestive system.

For All Digestive Issues

Check with Your Doctor

It's usually nothing serious but check with a gastroenterologist to make sure your symptoms aren't coming from Celiac Disease, Crohn's Disease, diverticulitis, colitis, hernias, or ulcers. They can also check for small intestinal bacterial overgrowth, or SIBO, which is less serious but possibly in need of antibiotic treatment, if you aren't able to treat it with diet and lifestyle alone.

Chew Thoroughly

The food you eat needs to be chewed thoroughly enough for digestive enzymes to break it down. Undigested food can lead to bloating and Irritable Bowel Syndrome (IBS). If you have trouble slowing down, then refer back to Part Two.

Don't Eat When You're Not Hungry

If you're not hungry when you eat, then your body isn't prepared with digestive enzymes to break your food down. If you find it hard to wait until you're hungry, then refer back to Part Two.

Hydrate

Your gut needs to be hydrated in order to function properly, because water is the base of digestive juices. Your gut is constantly reabsorbing water back into your body, so you should stay hydrated. Refer back to Part Two to find out how much water you should be drinking.

Destress

Your body doesn't have a built-in response to relationship problems or deadlines at work. It responds to any type of stress as a life-threatening situation. It redirects blood flow away from your gut and towards your muscles so you can fight or run away. During a time of stress, the last thing your body cares about is digesting your lunch. Refer back to Part Two for tips on how to reduce stress

IBS And Bloating

A lot of times, cutting back on wheat, dairy, sugar, and caffeine will drastically reduce bloating and IBS. But if you still have problems, it's worth trying a low FODMAP diet. FODMAP stands for fermentable oligosaccharides, disaccharides, monosaccharides, and polyols. Those are the types of sugars in certain foods that are easily fermented by the bacteria in your gut. The byproduct of the fermentation process are gases and toxins that lead to bloating, pain, and IBS.

Avoiding high FODMAP foods reduces bloating and IBS, but make sure you also drink enough water, only eat when you're hungry, chew your food thoroughly, and relax. You don't have to follow a low FODMAP diet forever. Try it for a few weeks, then reintroduce one high FODMAP food at a time.

Don't take probiotics or fermented foods until your symptoms are resolved. And be careful about hidden high FODMAP ingredients, like garlic in spices and supplements.

HIGH FODMAP FOODS TO AVOID

FRUITS	GRAINS	OTHER
Avocado, apples, apricots, blackberries, boysenberries, cherries, dates, figs, guava, goji berries, grapefruit, lychee, mangoes, nectarines, papaya, peaches, prunes, watermelon, pears, plums, dried fruit	Wheat, barley, or rye containing products ie: bread, cereal, pasta, baked goods egg noodles, almond meal, amaranth flower, gnocchi, couscous	Sorbitol, xylitol, chewing gum and low calorie or no sugar added products, high fructose corn syrup, honey, agave, cashews, pistachios, FOS, inulin, rum, jelly, pesto, falafel, hummus, relish, tahini, carob powder

| | MEAT | |
| | Chorizo, sausage | |

VEGETABLES	BEVERAGES	DAIRY
Asparagus, artichokes, beans, cauliflower, garlic, onions, mushrooms, sugar snap peas, tomato paste, sweet potato, celery, scallions	Dairy, whey protein, chai tea, dandelion tea, fennel tea, chamomile tea, oolong tea, more than one glass of wine or beer	All dairy products, ie: cheese, milk, ice cream, kefir, yogurt, frozen yogurt, sour cream

Acid Reflux

You can find relief from acid reflux if you lose weight and avoid overeating but check with your doctor to make sure that you don't have an infection from H. pylori, or a structural issue in your stomach.

Your doctor might recommend reflux medication, but that can do more harm than good. Reflux medication reduces stomach acid, which helps you feel better initially. But stomach acid is what keeps the sphincter in your esophagus tightly closed off from your stomach. Lowering the acid in your stomach with medication can actually loosen that sphincter and allow stomach acid to leak into your esophagus. The other problem with reducing acid with medication, is that you need enough acid to kill off unhealthy bacteria and digest your food. Do what you can to control your symptoms naturally. The best way to reduce reflux is to relax and avoid overeating. But you should also try to:

- Reduce wheat, dairy, and caffeine consumption.

- Drink a cup of water 10 minutes before you eat to hydrate the layer under your stomach that neutralizes acid.

- Drink teas like Throat Coat from Traditional Medicinals or Throat Comfort from Yogi. They have mucilaginous herbs that protect your esophagus from acid. It'll alleviate symptoms but won't solve any underlying causes of acid reflux like stress or overeating.

Don't Drink Your Calories

Soda, juices, sports drinks and flavored coffees are packed with sugar that absorbs quickly in your blood to be stored as fat. And they aren't filling.

If you love smoothies and make them often, use as little fruit in them as possible. Try using one frozen banana or mango because they're sweeter than most fruits and give a smooth texture. You can also add a packet of stevia for natural sweetness without added calories.

Consider Limiting Alcohol

Alcohol is about 100 calories per serving. And by one serving I mean 12 oz of beer, 5 oz of wine, and a 1 ½ oz shot of liquor. If you add juice or soda to the mix then you'll end up having hundreds of extra calories before the night is over. The calories from alcohol aren't added into any of the meal plans, but you can swap out the calories from snacks or the carb part of your meal.

Drinking isn't helpful when you're trying to lose weight. You might want to consider reducing your intake or abstaining altogether. It lowers any inhibitions that would otherwise prevent you from eating pizza at all hours of the night. And having a hangover usually leads to greasy food cravings the next day. Drinking at night especially doesn't help when you're trying to stick to a fast.

Try limiting the number of drinks you have in one sitting. It helps to drink water or soda water with citrus fruit in between drinks. For health reasons, the general recommendation is no more than one drink a day for women, and two for men. If you want to cut out alcohol altogether, then I would recommend the book *Allen Carr's Quit Drinking Without Willpower: Be a happy nondrinker*. It helps you get rid of the desire to drink, which makes it much easier to quit or at least slow down.

Treat Yourself

Your body doesn't want you to lose fat. It wants to save it for energy for a time when there's no food available. **When you lose fat, survival mechanisms kick in that make you gain it back.**

A lot of it has to do with the hormone leptin. Leptin gets released by fat cells. When you lose fat, you lose leptin. When your brain senses a drop in leptin, it increases your appetite and makes you feel lazy so that you eat more and burn less calories. It wants you to regain those emergency fat stores.

Fortunately, regaining weight is not the only way to restore leptin.

Having high carb cheat meals will actually raise leptin levels. That'll periodically suppress your appetite and give you more energy as you lose weight.

This is not to say that you should go all out. You can end up ruining all your progress. Your weight loss plans will show you how to cheat safely. You can get your calorie target for cheat days in Part Five on Calorie Targets. Not everyone needs to count calories, but it's good to know your target and limits.

Take Breaks

Most people try to lose weight all in one shot. But that usually doesn't work. They either gain the weight back, or they lose motivation before they hit their goal. As I mentioned, losing fat and therefore leptin will make you hungry and lazy.

Taking periodic breaks from weight loss will restore leptin levels and prevent your metabolism from slowing down. Research shows that these breaks help you maintain your new weight and can help you lose weight even faster. We'll go over how and when to take them in Part Eight.

Reduce Stress

Stress makes you more likely to overeat and crave junk food. But that's not the only issue. The hormones triggered by stress make you store fat more easily. And they interfere with the process that breaks down fat for energy. **So, stress makes it easier to gain weight, and harder to lose weight. Even if it's not making you eat more.** For more on stress reduction, refer back to Part Two.

Exercise

Exercise is a good way to burn calories and trigger fat loss. You don't have to exercise to lose weight, but it'll speed up the process. Cardio exercise like running is good for burning fat and glycogen stores. While strength training preserves and builds muscle as you lose weight. The more muscle you have, the better, because muscle cells burn a lot of calories. We'll cover more on exercise in Part Six.

Part Four

Weight Loss Plans

"Donuts are bad for you. And according to my health-nut wife, they're not appropriate for a trail mix. I'm just on a different trail, right? Mine leads to the emergency room"

-Jim Gaffigan

The key to losing weight is having a plan that's sustainable for *you*. Not everyone can fast for 16 hours a day, and some people will never log their calories in an app. There's an option here for everyone.

All the plans will result in weight loss, but Plan Four is ideal. It combines the benefits of hitting your caloric sweet spot with the benefits of being in a fasted state. But it's not ideal if it's not sustainable for you. Read through each plan to see how they're done. Then you can decide which one sounds like the best fit for you. If the plan isn't working for you, or if you want to try something new, then feel free to try a different plan.

As a reminder, these plans don't *just* refer to weekdays. A lot of people act like calories don't exist on the weekend. They tell me that they're sticking to the plan every day, so they don't understand why they didn't lose weight. But come to find out, they were going all out on the weekend.

However, you can decide to have your cheat days or cheat meals on the weekend. When and how to cheat are included in each plan. But it's not a free for all. You can easily ruin all your progress from the week by going overboard Friday to Sunday. If your schedule is different on the weekend, then you can choose a different plan for those days.

For example, Plan One could work well for you during the week because you're up too early to fast and you're so busy at work that you don't even have time for cravings. But Plan Three could work better on the weekends, because waking up late makes it easy to fast until lunch. Then you can save the calories you didn't have at breakfast for a more indulgent dinner.

Plan One
Balanced Slow-Carb

This plan doesn't rely on calorie tracking, meal plans, or fasting. But it does rely on you to follow your hunger and fullness signals, and choose meals that are balanced with vegetables, lean protein, and slow carbs.

If you're looking for more indulgent meals and snacks then you're more likely to stick with Plans Two, Three, or Four. **If you have no trouble eating balanced, slow carb meals for most of your diet, then this might be the plan for you**. You can still eat balanced slow carb meals with attention to hunger and fullness in the other plans. But this plan requires the most adherence to those rules.

Keep in mind that this isn't foolproof. It's entirely possible to eat too many calories, even if you're having healthy balanced meals. Especially if you don't cook them yourself. If you take a look at the calories at some restaurants, you might be surprised to see that your big plate of vegetables is actually over 800 calories. That's more than you'll get from a Double Quarter Pounder with cheese. That might be the right amount of food for some of you, but not everyone.

It's a good idea to at least find out what your calorie target is. Take a look at the amount of calories in your food, even if you're not going to track them.

Keep track of your weight closely to make sure that you're losing about half a pound to two pounds a week. If you're losing weight too quickly or too slowly, then follow Plan Two for at least a couple of days, to get an idea of how much you should be eating.

The Upside
- No effort or restriction of calorie counting or fasting every day.
- You may find that you eat healthier, because your restrictions are based on the quality of the food you eat as opposed to calories.

The Downside
- It'll take more discipline to stick to specific foods on a daily basis
- It might take some trial and error to eat the right amount for a healthy rate of weight loss

How To Follow Plan One
1. Eat meals that are balanced with lean protein, slow carbs, and non-starchy vegetables.
2. Always eat when you start to feel hungry.
3. Don't eat when you're not hungry.
4. Chew your food thoroughly.
5. Stop eating when you're comfortably full.
6. Preferably eat within a 12-hour window every day.
7. Track your weight closely.
8. If you're losing weight too quickly or too slowly then follow Plan Two for at least two days to get an accurate sense of how much you should be eating.

Choose A Way to Cheat
- Have a 50 to 200 calorie treat daily.
- Have a cheat meal once a week.

Plan Two
Calorie Control

To lose weight, it's always best to hit your caloric sweet spot. If you don't eat enough, you'll slow down in your metabolism and an increase in your appetite. If you eat *too much*, then you won't lose weight. Hitting your calorie target does require a little more effort than Plan One. But that effort is worth the consistent weight loss and flexibility when it comes to your food choices. You can budget your calories however you want.

For this plan, you'll be using an app to log your calories, following a meal plan, following a calorie guide per meal, or a combination of all three.

The Upside
- This plan gives you a lot of flexibility if you're not ready to give up junk food. As long as they fit into your calories without leaving you hungry, you can still lose weight.
- No fasting.
- Logging your intake will start to become a habit, and it only takes a minute or two each day.
- Eating a consistent amount of calories on a daily basis will give you consistent weight loss.
- You'll probably be surprised to see how much you can actually eat. Some people are going far under calories just to "be good." But they end up being hungry and overeating the next day.
- Seeing the caloric load of different foods can help you decide if they're worth it or not.

The Downside
- Tracking calories or following a meal plan requires some effort and attention to detail.

How To Follow Plan Two
1. Figure out your calorie target by referring to Part Five: Calorie Targets.
2. Eat that amount of calories on a daily basis by logging calories with an app, using a meal plan, a calorie guide per meal, or a combination of all three. See Part Five on *How To Hit Your Calorie Target* for more detail.
3. Don't eat less than your calorie target to lose weight faster, or you'll slow down your metabolism and halt your weight loss.
4. Always eat when you start to feel hungry.
5. Don't eat when you're not hungry.
6. Chew your food thoroughly.
7. Stop eating when you're comfortably full.
8. As much as you can, eat balanced meals with lean protein, slow carbs, and non-starchy vegetables. It'll help to preserve muscle, keep you full, and improve your health and mood. But it's not absolutely necessary as long as you're hitting your calorie target.

Choose A Way to Cheat
- Have one day a week that you don't track your meals or follow a meal plan.
- A weekly cheat meal, while still hitting your weight loss calorie target.
- Once a week, go above your weight loss calorie target. See Part Five for your cheat day calorie target.
- Fit in a daily treat, while still hitting your weight loss calorie target every day.

Plan Three
Intermittent Fasting

There's no calorie tracking with this plan, but you'll have to spend 16 hours of the day without eating. But those 16 hours do include the time that you're asleep. It's really only a few hours without eating, at the beginning and end of the day. Fasting depletes your body's stored glycogen, which allows you to start using fat as a fuel source. So, you'll be spending a few hours each day in a fat burning state. **Fasting also improves your health by promoting detoxification, DNA repair, metabolic and cardiac health, and stem cell generation.**

Sixteen hours might seem like a long time to go without eating. But it's actually easy to do after about a week, when your body gets used to the routine. Fasting affects everyone differently, so don't continue with the plan if you're feeling very tired or agitated. Studies even show that fasting affects men and women differently. Possibly because we're mostly evolved from men who were hunting all day, and women who were at home taking care of children. Women needed to maintain their fat stores in order to bear children and feed them. It doesn't mean that women can't fast, it just means that you should experiment to find what feels good for you.

The Upside
- No calorie counting or following meal plans.
- Having a cut off time can make it easier to avoid late night snacks.
- There are many health benefits of being in a fasted state.

The Downside
- You can potentially be undereating, which can cause your weight loss to plateau too early.
- You have less time in the day for eating.

- There's a potential for cravings after not eating for a few hours, but this doesn't happen to everyone. Especially if you continue to drink water when you're hungry during your fast.

How To Follow Plan Three
1. Pick an 8-hour eating window during your waking hours, leaving 16 consecutive hours for fasting. Fasting time includes the time that you're asleep.
2. Start off slowly, with one day a week of fasting. Then work your way up to five to seven days a week. If 16 hours is too long for you at first, then start with 12 hours and work your way up to 16.
3. Download the app Zero if you're having trouble keeping track of your fasting time.
4. During your fast, only have water, plain tea, black coffee, or apple cider vinegar mixed with water.
5. Drink water whenever you *start* to feel hunger, during your fast. It'll keep you from getting too hungry.
6. During your eating window, always eat when you start to feel hungry, and avoid eating when you're not hungry.
7. Chew your food thoroughly.
8. Stop eating when you're comfortably full.
9. During your eating window, eat mostly balanced meals with lean protein, slow carbs, and non-starchy vegetables.

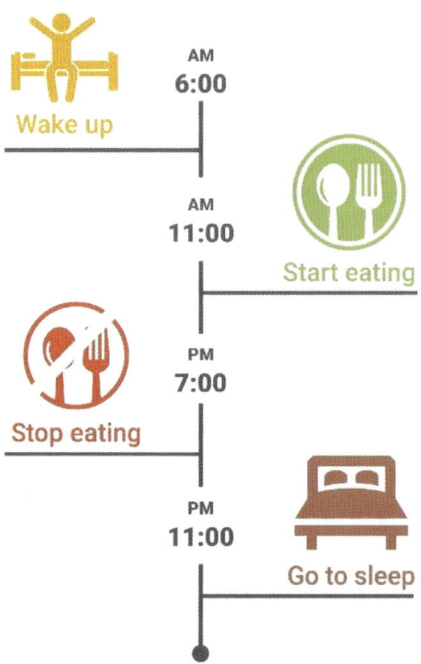

Choose A Way to Cheat
- Don't fast on one or two days of the week.
- Have one to two cheat meals a week, during your eating window.
- Have a small daily treat within your eating window.

Plan Four
Calorie Controlled Intermittent Fasting

This is the most effective plan for weight loss because you're combining the benefits of accurate calorie intake with the health and weight loss benefits of fasting. With this plan, your eating window can be more flexible. It can be anywhere from 10 hours to 4 hours long. Leaving you in a fasted state for 14 to 20 hours. Some days can be longer than others, if you choose. As long as you're hitting your calorie target.

The Upside
- No guesswork involved. You're sure to be getting in the right amount of calories with the added benefit of fasting.

The Downside
- Tracking calories or following a meal plan requires some effort and attention to detail.
- You have less time for eating.
- There's a potential for cravings after not eating for a few hours, but this doesn't happen to everyone. Especially if you continue to drink water when you're hungry during your fast.

How To Follow Plan Four
1. Figure out your calorie target by referring to Part Five: Calorie Targets.
2. Eat that amount of calories on a daily basis by logging calories with an app, using a meal plan, a calorie guide per meal, or a combination of all three. See Part Five on *How To Hit Your Calorie Target* for more detail.
3. Don't eat less than your calorie target to lose weight faster, or you'll slow down your metabolism and halt your weight loss.

4. Pick a 10 to 4 hour eating window during your waking hours, leaving 14 to 20 consecutive hours for fasting. Fasting time includes sleep.
5. Start off slowly, with one day a week. Then work your way up to five to seven days a week. If the fasting time you choose is too long for you at first, then start with a shorter time, and work your way up.
6. Download the app Zero if you're having trouble keeping track of your fasting time.
7. During your fast, only have water, plain tea, black coffee, or apple cider vinegar mixed with water.
8. Drink water whenever you *start* to feel hungry, during your fast. It'll keep you from getting too hungry.
9. During your eating window, always eat when you start to feel hungry, and avoid eating when you're not hungry.
10. Chew your food thoroughly.
11. Stop eating when you're comfortably full.
12. As much as you can, eat balanced meals with lean protein, slow carbs, and non-starchy vegetables. It'll help to preserve muscle, keep you full, and improve your health and mood. But it's not absolutely necessary as long as you're hitting your calorie target.

20:4 FAST EXAMPLE

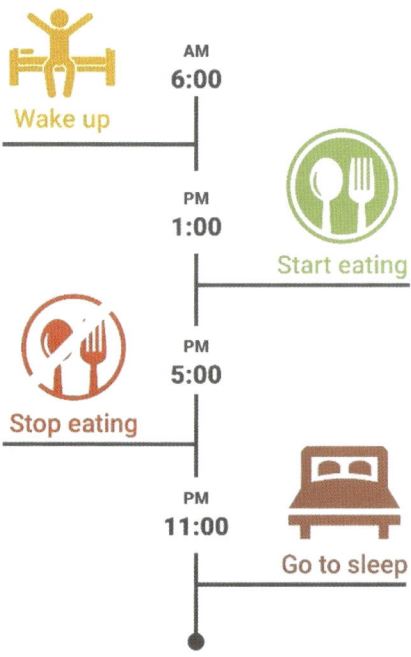

Choose A Way to Cheat
- Don't fast for one or two days but continue to hit your calorie target.
- Have one day a week of no fasting and eat more than your calorie target. See Part Five for your cheat day calorie target.
- Have one to two cheat meals a week, within eating window, without going over your weight loss calorie target.
- Have a small daily treat within eating window and calorie range.

Plan Five
Balanced Slow-Carb with Weekly Fast

This plan is just like Plan One, but with a weekly weight loss boost. You'll **eat mostly balanced meals except for one day a week that you fast for the whole day.** You can start off with Plan One, and switch to this plan if you feel like you're not losing fast enough. Again, I would recommend that you follow Plan Two for at least a couple of days to get an idea of how much you should be eating based on your RMR.

The Upside
- No calorie counting or following meal plans.
- You get the health and weight loss benefits of fasting.
- You may find that you eat healthier, because your restrictions are based on the quality of the food you eat as opposed to calories.

The Downside
- A full day fast might be too much for some people to handle.
- There's a potential for cravings after not eating for many hours, but this doesn't happen to everyone. Especially if you continue to drink water when you're hungry during your fast.

How To Follow Plan Five
1. Pick one day a week to fast for a full day.
2. On fasting days, drink only water, plain tea, black coffee, or apple cider vinegar mixed with water.
3. Drink water whenever you start to feel hungry during your fast.
4. On non fasting days, don't overly restrict. But eat mostly balanced meals with lean protein, slow carbs, and non starchy vegetables.

5. On non fasting days, eat when you start to feel hungry and stop when you're comfortably full.
6. It's not necessary, but it's beneficial to eat within a 12 hour window on non fasting days.

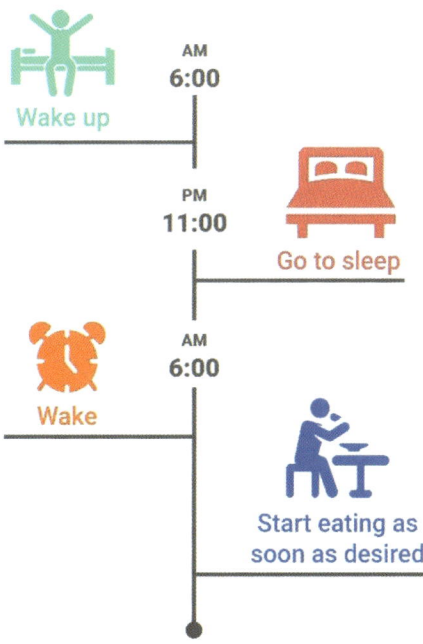

Choose A Way to Cheat
- Have a 100 to 200 calorie treat daily.
- Have a weekly cheat meal.

Plan Six
Bi-Weekly Calorie Controlled Fast

For this plan, you'll pick two days a week to have only 500 calories towards the *end* of the day. You'll be fasting for about 20 hours on both of those days. For the other five days, you'll be eating mostly balanced meals.

The Upside
- No calorie counting or following meal plans on non-fasting days.
- You get the health and weight loss benefits of fasting.
- You may find that you eat healthier, because your restrictions are based on the quality of the food you eat as opposed to calories.

The Downside
- Two long fasts a week might be too much for some people to handle.
- There's a potential for cravings after not eating for many hours, but this doesn't happen to everyone. Especially if you continue to drink water when you're hungry during your fast.

How To Follow Plan Six
1. Pick two days a week for fasting.
2. On fasting days, eat 500 calories towards the end of the day.
3. During your fasting window, drink only water, plain tea, black coffee, or apple cider vinegar mixed with water.
4. Drink water whenever you start to feel hunger, during your fast.
5. On non-fasting days, don't overly restrict. But try for balanced meals with lean protein, slow carbs, and non-starchy vegetables.
6. On non-fasting days, eat when you start to feel hungry and stop when you're comfortably full.

7. It's not necessary but it's beneficial to eat within a 12 hour window on non fasting days

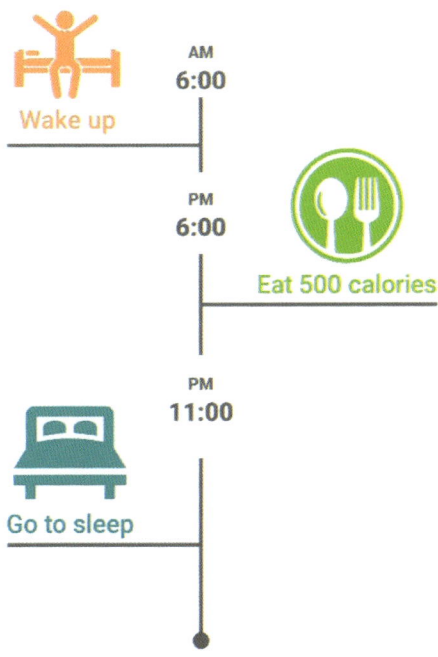

Choose A Way to Cheat
- Have cheat foods for the 500 calories on fasting days.
- Have a 100 to 200 calorie treat on non-fasting days.
- Have a weekly cheat meal on a non-fasting day.

Part Five

Calorie Targets

"No one admits to going to McDonald's. They sell six billion hamburgers a day. There's only 300 million people in this country. It's like, 'Hmm I'm not a calculus teacher, but I think everyone's lying'"

-Jim Gaffigan

Get Your Weight Loss Calorie Target

This section applies to those of you who chose Plans Two and Four. But like I've said, it's a really good idea for everyone to get a sense of their weight loss calorie target.

The best way to determine your calorie target is with your resting metabolic rate, or RMR. Your RMR is the amount of energy from food or "calories" your body needs for vital functions like breathing, temperature control, and circulating your blood. Eating this amount will keep your metabolism from slowing down as you lose weight.

The gold standard for measuring RMR is indirect calorimetry, but you need expensive tools and people who know how to use them. It's not the most practical way to find it. Instead, you can use math. But you don't have to do it yourself; there're online calculators to do it for you.

How To Find Your RMR

There're a few equations that estimate your RMR. **The most accurate equations are based on your body composition.** Meaning the ratio of fat to muscle in your body.

Muscle cells burn more energy than fat cells. Someone who's 200 pounds with 150 pounds of muscle will burn more calories than someone who's the same weight but has only 70 pounds of muscle.

It would be ideal if you could buy or use a handheld body fat monitor or scale to get your body fat percent. I would recommend either of these:

- RENPHO Bluetooth Body Fat Scale
- OMRON Handheld Body Fat Loss Monitor

If you have your body fat percent, then you can plug that and your weight into my online calculator in the meal plans section of my website (crkwellness.com), or you can do it yourself with the equation below.

Katch-McArdle Equation

RMR= 370 + 21.6 x Lean Body Mass in kg

If you *don't* have your body fat percent, you can still get your RMR. It might not be as accurate but it's very close. To get your RMR without body fat percent, use the Mifflin St. Jeor equation below. It's a complicated equation so use my online calculator in the meal plans section of my website (crkwellness.com).

Mifflin St. Jeor Equation

Men	10 x weight (kg) + 6.25 x height (cm) – 5 x Age + 5
Women	10 x weight (kg) + 6.25 x height (cm) – 5 x Age – 161

Now That You Know Your RMR

Use your RMR as your daily calorie target. In the next section I'll show you how to make sure you're hitting it every day.

Your RMR might be more than you'd think you should have. But if you eat less than your RMR you'll slow your metabolism down before you reach your goal.

Or you might feel like your RMR is too low. If you're very active or if you're used to eating a lot more than that, it can be too restrictive. But you'll know it's not enough food if you're losing more than two

pounds a week, if you're waking up very hungry, or if you're hungry in the middle of the night.
If you feel that your calorie target is too low then add on 100 calories to your daily calorie target and trial that for a week and see if that's enough. If you still need more, than trial another 100 calories more.

It's also possible that your estimated RMR is too high.

If you aren't losing weight with your calorie target, you can adjust by reducing 100 calories from your calorie target and trialing that for a week.

We'll discuss how to manage weight fluctuations more in Part Seven.

Adjust Calorie Target to Weight Loss

Your RMR will drop slightly as you lose weight. Recalculate your RMR for every ten pounds you lose.

Cheat Day Calorie Targets

Sometimes on cheat days, you'll be eating more than your daily calorie target. But you don't want to eat *too* much. **You should be eating the amount of calories that would maintain your weight.** Which is your RMR multiplied by 1.2. Eating more than that will cause weight gain.

Below are the cheat day calorie targets for 1200 to 2400 calorie diets. For example, if your daily calorie target for weight loss is 1500 calories, then you can have up to 1800 calories on a cheat day without gaining weight.

If you go over your cheat day calorie target, it won't ruin everything.

WEIGHT LOSS CALORIE TARGET	CHEAT DAY CALORIE TARGET
1200	1440
1300	1560
1400	1680
1500	1800
1600	1920
1700	2040
1800	2160
1900	2280
2000	2400
2100	2520
2200	2640
2300	2760
2400	2880

But it's worth keeping track of.

Exercise Calories

Your calorie target will stay the same, regardless of the calories you burn from exercise. *Unless* **you're exercising so much that it's just not enough food for you. Or if you're losing more than two pounds every week.** Then it's okay to eat a little more. Or you could just work out less.

You might notice that the calories you burn from walking or exercising will change your remaining calories if your using an app like MyFitnessPal. **If you eat more to compensate for those calories, you're just wasting the calories you burned during your workout.** The extra calories you burned could be helping you lose weight faster. Your best bet is to un-sync the calories burned with exercise, in the app. Or just ignore it. Especially because studies show that none of those smart devices are accurate enough to rely on when it comes to estimating calories burned.

How To Hit Your Calorie Target

There are a few different ways to make sure you're hitting your calorie target. You can **track your food in an app, follow a guideline of calories for each meal, use a meal plan, or do a combination of all three.**

Some of my patients just follow their meal plan, knowing that it hits their target. So they don't bother tracking. I make the plans as realistic as possible, even if it means they're eating eggs for dinner. I always give them some lazy options, because life's not perfect.

Even with lazy options, some people will follow their meal plan sometimes, but not always. Which is fine. They'll eat the breakfast on the plan, but then eat something different for lunch. Each meal on their plan shows calories. So, they'll log the calories from breakfast, and then track whatever else they eat for the rest of the day, until they hit their target.

The plans have a few different options for every meal and snack, so it's not as if they're eating the same thing every day. But even with options, some people don't like to follow a meal plan at all. They'll log the calories of everything they eat until they hit their target. To make it easy, they eat from restaurants that post calories, choose recipes that show calories, or use meal services like Freshly that post calories. Or they eat some of the same things on a regular basis, and save the calories of those meals in the app. That way they don't have to figure it out more than once.

That's the way I do things. I skip breakfast and I fast until lunch, which I get from Fresh & Co, Just Salad, Cava, The Little Beet, or Indikitchen. All good quality, very tasty food, lots of vegetable options, and they all post calories. I'll snack on a fruit, which is always easy to log. And for dinner I use a recipe that shows calories. Or I'll order one of my go-to dinners, like chicken and broccoli from the Chinese place (or General Tso's if I have 800 calories left). I've already looked up those meals, so it's easy to track them. For dessert, I've got a stash of Dove chocolates in the fridge. Four for 150 calories. Easy, tasty, mostly healthy, and always hits my target.

Meal Plans

If you prefer to cook most of your meals, then you can use the free meal plans on my website (crkwellness.com). There are meal plans for calorie targets between 1200 and 2400 calories.

One set of plans include breakfast, lunch, dinner, and snack options. The second set is for intermittent fasting plans, so they don't include breakfast. The calories leftover from breakfast are spread throughout the other meals and snacks.

Each plan has easy to follow recipes with leftovers, so that you don't have to cook every day. They also include an option to build meals from your choice of protein, carbs, vegetable, and sauces. You just pick one from each category and measure it out to the indicated portion size.

The recipes don't account for every single preference or dietary restrictions, so feel free to set up a session through my site if you'd like a more personalized plan. Otherwise you can follow any other plan of your choosing that hits your calorie target.

Calorie Guidelines

Instead of having to track everything you eat, you can follow the calorie guidelines on my website (crkwellness.com) for meals and snacks. This works best for people who usually get their food from restaurants that post calories.

You can check the menu for foods that hit your calorie target per meal or snack. Or you can search for recipes of foods that hit your calorie target.

These aren't strict guidelines, but you should try to spread out your calories evenly throughout the day. You can still track these calories in an app to make sure you don't lose track.

Tip: Check the website of the restaurant if you do not see the calories posted on the menu

Track Your Food

Having to log everything you eat might seem unnatural to you, but we're not living in a natural world. If you were living in nature, then there wouldn't be calorie dense man-made foods or even enough food available to make you fat in the first place. Living in an unnatural world, we have to do unnatural things to survive, like tracking our food.

There are a handful of calorie tracking apps and they all have their pros and cons. **The app that stands out the most is MyFitnessPal.** It's free, the easiest to use, and has the largest database of food.

But you should **use the calorie target that you calculated from your RMR.** Many times, the app will calculate a goal that's too low or too high.

If you track your calories there's no guesswork. You don't have to wonder if you ate too much, or if it's safe to have an extra cookie. It's the absolute best way to consistently lose weight.

Just make sure that you **check the calories of the food and make sure that you have calories remaining, b*efore* you eat it.**

For example:

You start the day with 1500 calories to spend. You log breakfast which is:

2 eggs: 160 calories
1 slice of bread: 80 calories
1 banana: 90 calories

Total: 330 calories

Now you have 1,170 calories left for lunch and dinner.

At lunch, you head over to Subway and scan the menu for a sandwich. That's the time you want to check the calories.

If you just eat a footlong Meatball Marinara and log it afterwards then you'll be left with only 150 calories for dinner.

Instead you might decide to get a 6" Meatball Marinara for half the calories, leaving you with 665 calories for the rest of the day. That's enough for dinner and maybe even dessert.

If you don't want to log calories, then be honest with yourself. It could be that you're feeling too lazy or that you don't have time. But it only takes a few seconds and it's not hard to do.

The real reason is probably that you don't want to know how much you're eating. You just eat what you think will hit your target and hope for the best. But you're better off knowing how many calories are in your food. Otherwise it's way too easy to lie to yourself and eat more than you should be. Or overestimate how much you ate and skip dessert for no reason. So, don't make excuses for yourself.

Tracking is easy but it *can* get a little more tedious if you don't use recipes or eat from restaurants that post calories. But the app has a huge database of food, so you can find it even if the calories aren't posted.

For example, I go to the diner sometimes for a Belgian waffle sundae. The diner doesn't post those calories, but I figured it out in one minute, and saved it in the app for next time. I looked up each part separately, using visual comparisons to judge the portion sizes. I'll go over those in a minute.

1 Belgian waffle: 300 calories
1 cup of vanilla ice cream: 240 calories
2 oz maple syrup: 147 calories
½ cup of whipped cream: 77 calories

That's 764 calories altogether. Not bad. It leaves me just over 500 for dinner. The perfect amount for a big bowl of sweet potatoes and vegetables with chipotle lime dressing.

If you can measure the portion of food instead of using visual comparisons, it would be even better. Having a small kitchen scale makes it easy. Scales work best for proteins that are hard to pack into a measuring cup, but they work well for anything. And it keeps you from having to wash measuring cups or spoons. You can keep one at home and at work.

Just make sure that you:

- Put the plate or container on the scale first, then hit "tare" to bring the weight back to zero. Or place the plate or container on the scale before you turn it on. This will keep you from accidentally adding the weight of the plate or container to the weight of the food.

- Keep the scale on a flat surface while you're weighing.

There'll be times that don't have a scale, but you can use visual comparisons below to make a good estimate.

If your food has a package, then you can just scan the barcode in the app and adjust the portion size.

VISUAL PORTION SIZE COMPARISON

3" BAGEL

PORTION VISUAL: HOCKEY PUCK

1 CUP FRUITS AND VEGETABLES

PORTION VISUAL: 1 FIST

3 OZ MEAT AND FISH

PORTION VISUAL: DECK OF CARDS

1 CUP GRAINS, BEANS

PORTION VISUAL: FIST

1.5 OZ CHEESE

PORTION VISUAL: 4 DICE

2 TBS NUT BUTTER, OILS

PORTION VISUAL: SHOT GLASS

1 OZ NUTS

PORTION VISUAL: HAND FULL

½ CUP ICE CREAM

PORTION VISUAL: 2 PING PONG BALLS

4" DIAMETER PANCAKE

PORTION VISUAL: COMPACT DISK

Part Six

Exercise

"I exercised once but found that I was allergic to it. My skin flushed and my heart raced. I got sweaty and short of breath. Very dangerous."

-Reader's Digest

You don't have to exercise to lose weight, but it helps. If you decide to add in exercise, then you should do a combination of cardio and strength training. **Cardio helps you burn more calories and strength training will maintain your muscle. It's important to preserve muscle as you lose weight, because muscle burns calories.** If you don't do any strength training, then you'll likely lose muscle as you lose weight.

I'm not a personal trainer but I'm a Sensei of Judo and Jiu Jitsu. I get all my advice from research and experts, but the advice here isn't in place of a trainer if you decide you want one. This is just a guide to help you get started.

General Exercise Tips

Find A Routine You Enjoy

You're not going to work out consistently if you hate doing it. So explore different apps, machines, and routines until you find a few that you like. It's fine to stick to those for a while, until they get easy or boring. Then you can switch it up with something new.

Keep Your Goal in Mind

When you're feeling too lazy to exercise, it's easy to forget why you're even doing it in the first place. Instead of just forcing yourself to work out, try to visualize how your body will look and how you'll feel from all your effort.

Start Off Slow

If you're lacking motivation to work out, then don't agonize about it. Set small goals for yourself, just to get in the habit. Or tell yourself that it's just this one time for a few minutes. Once you actually start the workout, you'll feel good from the endorphins that it triggers. You'll want to keep up the habit.

Set Up Triggers

Your reward center will remember the feeling it gets from a workout. You can trigger the craving for that feeling by leaving out your gym clothes or workout equipment. And you're more likely to exercise if you make the process as convenient as possible.

Hydrate

Always make sure you're hydrated before the workout and have water on you . Dehydration will cause you to burn out too quickly.

Stretch

Stretch after your workouts so that you're not too sore to exercise the next day. Hold each stretch for 20-30 seconds. Start the stretch gently, at a point where it doesn't cause discomfort. Then gradually stretch the muscle even further every few seconds, as it loosens.

Refuel

Refuel after workouts with water and at least a piece of fruit, if you're feeling hungry.

Try Not to Caffeinate

Pre workouts have caffeine and amphetamine-like compounds that can damage your blood vessels. Some of them have even been taken off the market because they've caused fatal heart conditions. Even just having coffee before a workout can be harmful. Caffeine restricts your blood vessels while you have blood pumping through them, which can cause damage.

Strength Training Tips

Breathe

Before you start, take a few deep breaths through your nose and out of your mouth. Once you start your workout, breathe *out* through your nose as you lift the weight or contract the muscle. Breathe *in* through your nose as you lower the weight or extend the muscle.

Use Your Head

While you do the exercise, focus your mind on the muscle that you're trying to strengthen. It'll keep you focused during the workout and maximize the benefit. Your muscles actually respond to your thoughts. It may seem crazy, but studies have shown that even without *any* physical movement, strength is developed through mental attention to the muscle, alone.

Increase Time Under Tension

Time under tension refers to how long your muscle is under strain during a set. Putting a muscle under strain for a longer time cases more muscle breakdown. In other words, slow down each set to 30-40 seconds each in order to increase muscle growth. Maintain a consistent tempo throughout the set, including the time that you're lowering the weight.

Rest

Give each muscle group at least one day of rest. And take at least one full rest day each week from exercise.

Answers to The Usual Questions

"How much weight should I use?"

If you're a beginner, you can just start with your body weight. Try squats, sit-ups, planks and push-ups. If that's not challenging enough then add in weights or resistance bands. If you're training with weights, use a weight that challenges you, without sacrificing your form. It should be just enough so that your last rep is hard to finish.

Stick to the same workout routine and increase the weight by about 5 pounds as needed, or increase the number of reps as your muscles get stronger. For example, if you're able to do 15 reps and four sets of the workout with ease, then you're ready to go up in weight.

"How long should I work out for?"

Start off slowly, with one or two days a week for 20 minutes. Then work your way up. Aim for 10 to 15 reps and three sets of each exercise. It's not an exact science but it's a good place to start.

"Should I use workout supplements?"

In my opinion, no. I've yet to find a supplement that's well researched and has proven benefits. If anything, there are potential risks. Especially with pre workouts that have caffeine and amphetamine-like compounds. As for protein supplements, you can easily get enough through food. Supplements usually have calories you don't need, and extremely high concentrations of protein that strain your kidneys. And the protein you don't need gets stored as fat. If you want to use a protein supplement, I would recommend Vega Clean Protein for its quality ingredients.

Strength Training Apps

As I said, you can get a trainer to show you the ropes. But you don't need one. You can always just do the basics or use one of the apps below to help you come up with a routine.

Asics Studio
Price: Free to download, subscriptions vary
Mostly strength training, audio classes with playlists

PEAR
Price: Free to download, $5.99/month
Audio guided workouts from different trainers, including Olympians

Workout Tracker Gym Log
Price: Free
Workout tracker and weekly lifting plans

Sworkit
Price: Free
Body weight exercises

Runtastic Results
Price: Free
Personalized 12 week no-weight strength training plans for beginners

Nike+ Training Club
Price: Free
Workout tracking and 100+ workouts from Nike trainers, professionals, and celebrities

Daily Burn

Price: Free to download, $14.95 a month (includes a free 30-day trial)

Stream 800 routines, like dance cardio, yoga, or strength training.

Cardio Tips

Breathe

You can breathe through your nose if it's more comfortable, but you'll get more oxygen through your mouth. You'll find a rhythm that works best for you. Just avoid shallow breaths through your chest while you run. Focus on deep breaths through your belly.

Don't Overdo It

You don't have to go crazy with cardio, just try to do anything that gets your heart rate up for about 20 minutes to an hour. Whether its walking, running, dancing or using the Stairmaster, the main goal is to keep a consistent, steady pace that's challenging.

High Intensity Interval Training

If you hate putting the time in for cardio, then try high intensity interval training. You'll burn the same amount of calories in less time.

An example of HIIT on the elliptical or treadmill is

1. 4 minute walking warm up
2. 15 minutes of alternating between running for 45 seconds then walking for 45 seconds
3. 4 minute walking cool down

Apps for Cardio and HIIT

HIIT Workouts By Daily Burn
Price: Free to download, $9.99/month for premium
10, 20, and 30 minute high-intensity interval training workouts

Interval Timer
Price: Free
Minimal timer, can be synced with Apple watch

12-Minute Athlete HIIT Workouts
Price: $2.99 to download, $4.99/month
12-minute high-intensity interval training (a.k.a. HIIT) workouts

Kineticoach
Price: Free
600+ custom time based workouts

Nike+ Training Club
Workout tracking and 100+ workouts from Nike trainers, professionals, and celebrities

Daily Burn
Price: Free to download, $14.95 a month (includes a free 30-day trial)
Stream 800 routines, like dance cardio, yoga, or strength training.

Part Seven

Weight and Body Composition

"I try to avoid things that make me fat like scales, mirrors and photographs"

-Unknown

Tracking Your Weight

Some of you might not want to, but **it's important to keep track of your weight.** Otherwise you won't know if your weight loss plan is working, or if you're making mistakes. If you don't keep track, you could easily be wasting your time. **You won't be able to track your progress based on how your pants fit or how fat your cheeks look.**

I have plenty of patients who think they can get away with this, and they're always surprised by their actual weight in my office. I have one patient who's lost 50 pounds and is so incapable of noticing the change in his body that he accused me of tampering with the scale.

Then there are others who refuse to believe they *haven't* lost weight. Even if the scale shows the same number every week. They convince themselves that they've been following the plan even though they admit to indulging in off-the-plan chips and cookies every day.

Body dysmorphia is a real thing. Your mind is very good at playing tricks on you, so let the numbers be the judge.

Some people can't stand to check their weight because of the emotion it brings up. But you shouldn't use that as an excuse. If seeing your weight makes you unhappy, then you should work on how you talk to yourself about your weight.

Not everyone is afraid of the scale, though. There are some people who weigh themselves three times a day and obsess over every number. But there's no need to obsess about small weight fluctuations, because they're completely normal. **Your weight can fluctuate a few pounds a day from food and water retention. It doesn't mean that you actually gained body fat.**

You should expect to see your weight rise and fall throughout the day and the week. **Your weight won't drop steadily every day**. Some days it'll even look like you gained weight, but then the next day, you'll hit a new low number. There might only be one day in the week that you're a pound or two less than you were the week before. You should weigh yourself every morning so that you don't miss seeing that new low number. If you only check your weight every once in a while, you won't have a good sense of your progress.

Keep a scale somewhere convenient like the bathroom, so you can weigh yourself every day without clothes on.

If You Don't See Change

If you weren't eating enough before you started your weight loss plan, then you probably won't see a new low number in the first week or two. Your metabolism has to get used to having enough food. But, once your body gets used to it, the weight will come off easily. And menstruating women should keep in mind that your weight can go up a few pounds before and during your cycle, from water retention.

Don't expect your weight to drop every day. You can expect to see the scale drop by two pounds one day and go up even a few pounds the next. It can stay up for a few days, even if you're doing all the right things. At that point it's important that you don't get discouraged and decide to fall off your diet, or overly restrict. Just keep it up and you'll see the weight come back down by the end of the week.

If your weight still hasn't come down after two weeks, then refer back to the plan. Make sure there isn't something you're missing. Make sure you're tracking your food accurately. If you're sure that you're not missing anything or miscalculating calories, then it's possible that you need to switch plans to something that your body responds to more positively.

Or you may need to experiment by dropping your calorie target by 100 calories, and trialing that for one week.

You might also see a plateau if you're building muscle with strength training exercises. That's why it's important to keep track of your body composition as you lose weight. We'll cover this in more detail in the next part of this section.

If You Want to Lose Weight Faster

If you're losing a pound a week, and you'd rather lose two pounds a week, then don't just eat less. Make sure you're hitting your calorie target. Not eating enough will slow down your metabolism and increase your appetite. If you want to lose weight faster, then add in some cardio and strength training. Even walking for 30 minutes a day will help you burn hundreds of extra calories every week.

If You Lose Weight Too Quickly

If you're consistently losing more than two pounds a week, then you're not eating enough. You might get excited to see your weight drop, but I can assure you that you'll gain that weight back.

If you've been tracking your intake and hitting your calorie target, but still losing more than two pounds a week, then recalculate your daily calorie target. Make sure that you're accurately measuring portion sizes.

If you've been following a weight loss plan that doesn't require calorie control, then follow Plan Two for a few days to get a good sense of how much you should be eating for a healthy rate of weight loss.

Keep Track

It helps to keep track of your weight on paper, on an app like MyFitnessPal, or with a Bluetooth scale that automatically syncs your weight in an app. That way you can make sure you're losing at a healthy rate and figure out when it's time for a maintenance period. We'll cover those in Part Eight.

Make Sure Your Weights Are Accurate

1. Weigh yourself consistently without clothes and before you eat or drink in the morning.
2. Keep the scale on a flat surface.
3. Once you've found a flat surface, keep the scale in that spot.
4. If you suspect your weights are inaccurate then you might need to buy a new scale.
5. Don't skip weekends or days that you're afraid to see a high number.

Track Your Body Composition

There are a few reasons to keep track of your body composition

1. Muscle cells burn more calories than fat cells. So, you want to track your body composition to make sure that you aren't losing muscle as you lose weight. If you see that you're losing muscle, you can decide to add in some muscle building exercise and increase your protein intake.

2. If you're gaining muscle weight with exercise as you lose fat, then your weight might stay the same which could be discouraging. You would need to measure your body composition to make sure that you're losing fat.
3. Knowing your body composition will give you a more accurate RMR for your daily calorie target.

To measure your body composition, you can use a scale that measures body fat, a handheld body fat analyzer or have someone who's trained to use skin calipers measure it for you. If you belong to a gym, there'll most likely be staff members that are trained to use them. For your convenience, you can purchase either of these devices on Amazon.com through my website (crkwellness.com).

Products for Measuring Body Composition

RENPHO Bluetooth Body Fat Scale
OMRON Handheld Body Fat Loss Monitor

As you lose weight, your body fat percent should decrease *gradually*. It'll only be coming down a percent or two at a time. It's not something you should obsess about every day. Just check it every month, and for every 5 to 10 pounds you lose to make sure it's headed in the right direction.

To decrease your body fat percent more dramatically, you can add in or increase the amount of strength training you do as you lose fat.

If your weight is stable or increasing, but your body fat percent is decreasing, then you've lost fat and gained muscle. That's a good thing, so keep doing what you're doing.

If your body fat percent is increasing as you lose weight, then you're losing muscle. If that's the case, then make sure you're not eating less than your RMR, add in some muscle building exercises, and more protein rich foods to your diet.

The chart below can help you come up with a body fat percent goal. It's not something to obsess about, because everyone's body type is different. Just make sure that your body fat is gradually decreasing during weight loss.

RANGES OF BODY FAT PERCENTAGE

	MEN	WOMEN
Unhealthy	Less than 10-12%	Less than 2-4%
Athletic	14-12%	6-13%
Fit	21-24%	14-17%
Healthy	25-31%	18-25%
Obese	More than 32%	More than 26%

Part Eight

Weight Loss Breaks and Weight Maintenance

"He starts asking me about my eating patterns. Like there's habits, like there's a pattern. It's just chaos."

-Louis CK

Your body stores fat to use in case of emergencies. It has built in survival mechanisms to prevent you from losing it for good.

Your body responds to weight loss by slowing down your metabolism, and making you feel hungry and lazy which makes it impossible to keep the weight off.

But studies show that **taking periodic breaks from weight loss can prevent those survival mechanisms from kicking in.** That way you can lose the weight, without gaining it all back.

You need to take these breaks for every ten pounds you lose.

What I mean by "take a break," is adjust your intake so that you don't lose weight anymore. That doesn't mean you should *gain* weight. It means you should maintain it.

You'll maintain your weight for one to two weeks, and then go back to your weight loss plan. Until you reach your goal weight.

During your weight loss break you should weigh yourself every day to make sure you aren't gaining.

There are a few different ways to maintain your weight:

- If your weight loss plan is based on calories, then follow the weight maintenance calorie target guide below. If you're following a meal plan, then switch to the plan that'll hit your calorie target for weight maintenance.

- If your plan does *not* involve calorie control, then you can experiment by increasing your intake by a small amount at a time, until you see that your weight is stabilizing.

- If your weight loss plan is based on fasting, you can stop fasting for those two weeks. Or continue to fast, with your calorie target increased for maintenance.

- Instead of eating more, another option is to reduce or stop exercise for those two weeks.

After your maintenance period, return back to your previous weight loss plan.

Repeat weight loss breaks for every ten pounds you lose, until you hit your goal weight.

WEIGHT LOSS CALORIE TARGET	WEIGHT MAINTENANCE CALORIE TARGET
1200	1440
1300	1560
1400	1680
1500	1800
1600	1920
1700	2040
1800	2160
1900	2280
2000	2400
2100	2520
2200	2640
2300	2760
2400	2880

Once You've Hit Your Goal Weight

Once you hit your goal weight, it's easy to get lazy. But you don't want to be like the majority of people who gain back all the weight they've lost. It's easy to do, but it's avoidable.

Especially because **weight maintenance is less extreme than weight loss**. As you can see from the chart above, you need more calories for weight maintenance than weight loss. It takes less exercise and less frequent fasting. It'll be much easier to maintain this weight than it was to lose it.

But that doesn't mean you can drop all of your new habits. You don't have to fast or track your intake for the rest of your life. But you should continue to eat with your hunger signals, chew thoroughly, and eat *enough*.

Most importantly, you should continue to track your weight. A lot of people stop weighing themselves once they feel comfortable. And they don't get back on the scale until they feel fat. At that point, they've already gained five to ten pounds. If you keep track of your weight at least once a week, you'll notice if you go up a couple of pounds. At that point you can go back to your diet for just a week or two, to get back to your ideal weight.

Part Nine

Recap

"I wouldn't stop eating ice cream for anything. He said if you if you stop eating ice cream you'll live longer. I said give me another reason, that's not good enough"

-Louis CK

Now you have all the tools you need to lose weight. But that doesn't mean you'll retain everything. I'm not there with you to keep reminding you, so I'm giving you a quick recap to refer to. Hopefully it'll help it all sink in, if it hasn't already.

If you'd like me to help you through your weight loss journey, answer any questions, tweak your meal plan, keep you motivated and accountable, and provide a more personal guidance then feel free to set up a session through my website (crkwellness.com).

Final Recap

- Drink enough water to stay energized and prevent cravings.

- Meditate every day to stay calm. Stress is fattening.

- Get seven to nine hours of sleep each night. Getting less sleep than that will make you hungry.

- Take your time and chew your food thoroughly to prevent overeating.

- Stop eating when you're comfortably full.

- Only suppress your hunger signals while you're fasting.

- During your eating window, eat when you start to feel hungry. Don't let yourself get *too* hungry, or you'll overeat and slow down your metabolism.

- Don't eat if you're not hungry.

- Try to eat within a 12-hour window, while your metabolism is running.

- If you shorten your eating window to less than 12 hours, then your body will start to use fat for energy until you start eating again.

- Ideally, track your food or follow a meal plan to make sure you hit your calorie target. Undereating can cause quick weight loss, but you'll gain it back just as fast.

- Try to eat meals that are balanced with slow carbs, protein, and non-starchy vegetables.

- Treat yourself with cheat days, cheat meals, or a little treat every day. Just try not to go over your maintenance calorie target more than once a week.

- Remember that cravings are a trick that your reward center is playing on you. Don't tell yourself you can't have it. Just distract yourself and stop thinking about it until the craving disappears. If you want to fit it into your calories for the day, go ahead. No harm done. But continue to practice resisting whenever you can.

- Cleanse your palate with a mint, gum or breath spray as a meal ender. It'll keep you from craving something else.

- Keep some small treats around like a hard candy or small piece of chocolate to satisfy your sweet tooth without overindulging.

- If you're reaching to food to make yourself feel better, then work on your thoughts first. Negative thoughts trigger stress hormones and negative emotions, and they stop you from thinking clearly. Positive thoughts make you feel good and boost your brain function. So, choose wisely.

- Remember that healthy food boosts your mood and gives you all the materials your body needs to survive. Junk food is delicious, but it'll ruin your health and mood if you overdo it.

- Try healthier alternatives to junk food sometimes, when you're craving.

- Keep your gut healthy with enough fiber, water, exercise, and as little stress as you can manage. Try a probiotic if you don't have bloating. If you do experience chronic bloating, try a low FODMAP diet.

- Weigh yourself every day to make sure you're losing anywhere from a ½ a pound to 2 pounds a week on average.

- Keep track of your body composition to get an accurate calorie target, and to make sure you're not losing muscle.

- Exercise if you want to lose weight faster. And add in strength exercises if you're losing muscle.

- Take a one to two-week weight maintenance break for every ten pounds you lose. It'll prevent your metabolism from slowing down, and help you keep the weight off for good.

- Help yourself remember to drink water, meditate, etc., by making yourself a to do list, set alarms on your phone, or download the apps Do Less or Streaks.

References

Clinical Depression, g.co/kgs/ACnMGa.

Anxiety Disorder, g.co/kgs/ENpiyS.

Common Cold, g.co/kgs/k5nEh6.

Reynolds, S. (2011). *Happy Brain, Happy Life*. [online] Psychology Today. Available at: https://www.psychologytoday.com/us/blog/prime-your-gray-cells/201108/happy-brain-happy-life [Accessed 26 Apr. 2019].

Miller, MD, A. (2018). Five Things to Know About Inflammation and Depression. [online] Psychiatric Times. Available at: https://www.psychiatrictimes.com/special-reports/five-things-know-about-inflammation-and-depression [Accessed 21 Mar. 2019].

Pathak, Dipali. "12-Hour Biological Clock Coordinates Essential Bodily Functions". *Baylor College Of Medicine*, 2017, https://www.bcm.edu/news/molecular-and-cellular-biology/12-hour-clock-coordinates-bodily-functions.

Benton, David, and Hayley A. Young. "Reducing Calorie Intake May Not Help You Lose Body Weight". *Perspectives On Psychological Science*, vol 12, no. 5, 2017, pp. 703-714. *SAGE Publications*, doi:10.1177/1745691617690878. Accessed 21 Mar 2019.

Calatayud, Joaquin et al. "Importance Of Mind-Muscle Connection During Progressive Resistance Training". *European Journal Of Applied Physiology*, vol 116, no. 3, 2015, pp. 527-533. *Springer Nature*, doi:10.1007/s00421-015-3305-7. Accessed 21 Mar 2019.

Blomain, Erik Scott et al. "Mechanisms of Weight Regain following Weight Loss" *ISRN obesity* vol. 2013 210524. 16 Apr. 2013, doi:10.1155/2013/210524

"Adult Obesity." The Nutrition Source, 14 Apr. 2016, www.hsph.harvard.edu/obesity-prevention-source/obesity-trends/obesity-rates-worldwide/.

Byrne, N M et al. "Intermittent energy restriction improves weight loss efficiency in obese men: the MATADOR study" *International journal of obesity (2005)* vol. 42,2 (2017): 129-138.

Harvie, Michelle and Anthony Howell. "Potential Benefits and Harms of Intermittent Energy Restriction and Intermittent Fasting Amongst Obese, Overweight and Normal Weight Subjects-A Narrative Review of Human and Animal Evidence" Behavioral sciences (Basel, Switzerland) vol. 7,1 4. 19 Jan. 2017, doi:10.3390/bs7010004

Bouchez, Colette. "Serotonin and Depression: 9 Questions and Answers." WebMD, WebMD, www.webmd.com/depression/features/serotonin#1.

Lindseth, Glenda et al. "The effects of dietary tryptophan on affective disorders"*Archives of psychiatric nursing* vol. 29,2 (2014): 102-7.

Sears, Barry. "Anti-Inflammatory Diets." Journal of the American College of Nutrition, vol. 34, no. sup1, 2015, pp. 14–21., doi:10.1080/07315724.2015.1080105.

Kunnumakkara, Ajaikumar B et al. "Chronic diseases, inflammation, and spices: how are they linked?" Journal of translational medicine vol. 16,1 14. 25 Jan. 2018, doi:10.1186/s12967-018-1381-2

Fontana, Luigi and Linda Partridge. "Promoting health and longevity through diet: from model organisms to humans" *Cell* vol. 161,1 (2015): 106-118.

Mattson, Mark P. et al. "Impact Of Intermittent Fasting On Health And Disease Processes". *Ageing Research Reviews*, vol 39, 2017, pp. 46-58. *Elsevier BV*, doi:10.1016/j.arr.2016.10.005. Accessed 21 Mar 2019.

Altobelli, Emma et al. "Low-FODMAP Diet Improves Irritable Bowel Syndrome Symptoms: A Meta-Analysis" *Nutrients* vol. 9,9 940. 26 Aug. 2017, doi:10.3390/nu9090940

James W. Anderson, Pat Baird, Richard H. Davis, Jr, Stefanie Ferreri, Mary Knudtson, Ashraf Koraym, Valerie Waters, Christine L. Williams
Nutr Rev. 2009 Apr; 67(4): 188–205. doi: 10.1111/j.1753-4887.2009.00189.x

Lund University. "New link between gut bacteria and obesity." ScienceDaily. ScienceDaily, 23 February 2018. <www.sciencedaily.com/releases/2018/02/180223092441.htm>.

"Probiotic Supplements And Kombucha Review". *Consumerlab.Com*, 2019, https://www.consumerlab.com/reviews/Probiotic-Supplements-and-Kombucha-Drinks/probiotics/.

Davis, Cindy D. "The Gut Microbiome and Its Role in Obesity" *Nutrition today* vol. 51,4 (2016): 167-174.

Fontané, Laia, et al. "Influence of the Microbiota and Probiotics in Obesity." *Clínica e Investigación En Arteriosclerosis (English Edition)*, 2018, doi:10.1016/j.artere.2018.10.002.

Jenkins, David Ja, et al. "Glycemic Index: Overview of Implications in Health and Disease." The American Journal of Clinical Nutrition, vol. 76, no. 1, Jan. 2002, doi:10.1093/ajcn/76.1.266s.

Joseph, Mini et al. "Are Predictive Equations for Estimating Resting Energy Expenditure Accurate in Asian Indian Male Weightlifters?" Indian journal of endocrinology and metabolism vol. 21,4 (2017): 515-519.

Sabounchi, N S et al. "Best-fitting prediction equations for basal metabolic rate: informing obesity interventions in diverse populations" *International journal of obesity (2005)* vol. 37,10 (2013): 1364-70.

Miller, Robin. "Portion Control: Use Visual Cues to Remember Serving Sizes." Food Network, Food Network, 22 Feb. 2013, www.foodnetwork.com/healthyeats/2013/02/portion-control-use-visual-cues-to-remember-serving-sizes.

Riebl, Shaun K and Brenda M Davy. "The Hydration Equation: Update on Water Balance and Cognitive Performance" *ACSM's health & fitness journal* vol. 17,6 (2013): 21-28.

Gaiam. "1-Minute Breathing Exercise for Energy and Productivity." Gaiam, www.gaiam.com/blogs/discover/1-minute-breathing-exercise-for-energy-and-productivity.

Patel, Sanjay R. et al. "Association between Reduced Sleep and Weight Gain in Women." American journal of epidemiology 164.10 (2006): 947–954. PMC. Web. 26 July 2018.

Institute of Medicine (US) Committee on Sleep Medicine and Research; Colten HR, Altevogt BM, editors. Sleep Disorders and Sleep Deprivation: An Unmet Public Health Problem. Washington (DC): National Academies Press (US); 2006. 3, Extent and Health

Consequences of Chronic Sleep Loss and Sleep Disorders. Available from: https://www.ncbi.nlm.nih.gov/books/NBK19961/

Grandparents.com. "15 Science-Backed Ways To Fall Asleep Faster." The Huffington Post, TheHuffingtonPost.com, 29 Sept. 2016, www.huffingtonpost.com/entry/15-ways-to-fall-asleep-faster_us_55dde3e7e4b04ae497054470.

"The Mindful Way to Fall Asleep." Psychology Today, Sussex Publishers, www.psychologytoday.com/us/blog/the-land-nod/201408/the-mindful-way-fall-asleep.

Wolff, Carina. "7 Insomnia Cures That Sleep Experts Swear By." Bustle, Bustle, 13 Nov. 2018, www.bustle.com/p/7-insomnia-cures-that-sleep-experts-swear-by-9729309.

Tucker, Alexa. "10 Strength-Training Tips For Beginners That Will Make Your Workout More Effective." SELF, SELF, www.self.com/story/10-strength-training-tips-for-beginners-that-will-make-your-workout-more-effective.

Nóbrega, Sanmy R and Cleiton A Libardi. "Is Resistance Training to Muscular Failure Necessary?" Frontiers in physiology vol. 7 10. 29 Jan. 2016, doi:10.3389/fphys.2016.00010

Cava, Edda, et al. "Preserving Healthy Muscle during Weight Loss." Advances in Nutrition: An International Review Journal, vol. 8, no. 3, 2017, pp. 511–519., doi:10.3945/an.116.014506.

Romon, M., et al. "Leptin Response to Carbohydrate or Fat Meal and Association with Subsequent Satiety and Energy Intake." American Journal of Physiology-Endocrinology and Metabolism, vol. 277, no. 5, 1999, doi:10.1152/ajpendo.1999.277.5.e855.

Byrne, N M, et al. "Intermittent Energy Restriction Improves Weight Loss Efficiency in Obese Men: the MATADOR Study." International Journal of Obesity, vol. 42, no. 2, 2017, pp. 129–138., doi:10.1038/ijo.2017.206.

Zhang, Yuan, et al. "Angiopoietin-like Protein 8 (Betatrophin) Is a Stress-Response Protein That down-Regulates Expression of Adipocyte Triglyceride Lipase." Biochimica Et Biophysica Acta (BBA) - Molecular and Cell Biology of Lipids, vol. 1861, no. 2, 2016, pp. 130–137., doi:10.1016/j.bbalip.2015.11.003.

Luders, Eileen et al. "The unique brain anatomy of meditation practitioners: alterations in cortical gyrification" Frontiers in human neuroscience vol. 6 34. 29 Feb. 2012, doi:10.3389/fnhum.2012.00034

Luders, E, et al. "Forever Young(Er): Potential Age-Defying Effects of Long-Term Meditation on Gray Matter Atrophy." Deutsche Zeitschrift Für Akupunktur, vol. 58, no. 4, 2015, pp. 30–31., doi:10.1016/s0415-6412(15)30070-9.

Brewer, J. A., et al. "Meditation Experience Is Associated with Differences in Default Mode Network Activity and Connectivity." Proceedings of the National Academy of Sciences, vol. 108, no. 50, 2011, pp. 20254–20259., doi:10.1073/pnas.1112029108.

Mrazek, Michael D., et al. "Mindfulness Training Improves Working Memory Capacity and GRE Performance While Reducing Mind Wandering." Psychological Science, vol. 24, no. 5, May 2013, pp. 776–781, doi:10.1177/0956797612459659.

Goyal M, Singh S, Sibinga EMS, et al. Meditation Programs for Psychological Stress and Well-beingA Systematic Review and Meta-analysis. JAMA Intern Med. 2014;174(3):357–368. doi:10.1001/jamainternmed.2013.13018

Hölzel, Britta K et al. "Mindfulness practice leads to increases in regional brain gray matter density" Psychiatry research vol. 191,1 (2010): 36-43.

"7 Simple Mantras for Healing and Transformation." The Chopra Center, 8 Aug. 2018, chopra.com/articles/7-simple-mantras-for-healing-and-transformation.

"Meditation: Getting Started." OSHO | Meditation - Mindfulness and the Science of the Inner, www.osho.com/meditate/getting-started.

Volkow, Nora D et al. "Reward, dopamine and the control of food intake: implications for obesity" Trends in cognitive sciences vol. 15,1 (2010): 37-46.

Klosowski, Thorin. "Hack Your Brain to Use Cravings To Your Advantage." Lifehacker, Lifehacker.com, 24 June 2013, lifehacker.com/5887614/hack-your-brain-to-use-cravings-to-your-advantage.

"Weight Loss Motivation: Secrets to Staying on Track, Part 1." Psychology Today, Sussex Publishers, www.psychologytoday.com/us/blog/thriving101/201506/weight-loss-motivation-secrets-staying-track-part-1.

Anderson, Elizabeth and Geetha Shivakumar. "Effects of exercise and physical activity on anxiety" Frontiers in psychiatry vol. 4 27. 23 Apr. 2013, doi:10.3389/fpsyt.2013.00027

Harding, Jessica L, et al. "Psychosocial Stress Is Positively Associated with Body Mass Index Gain over 5 Years: Evidence from the Longitudinal AusDiab Study." Obesity, vol. 22, no. 1, 2013, pp. 277–286., doi:10.1002/oby.20423.

Mariotti, Agnese. "The effects of chronic stress on health: new insights into the molecular mechanisms of brain-body communication" Future science OA vol. 1,3 FSO23. 1 Nov. 2015, doi:10.4155/fso.15.21

Printed in Great Britain
by Amazon